# French Poems of the Great War

# French Poems of the Great War

## 102 Poems by 27 Poets

### Translated by Ian Higgins

Saxon Books

French Poems of the Great War

Translated by Ian Higgins

ISBN 978-0-9528969-9-9

Published by Saxon Books, 10 Bishops Place, Hurstpierpoint, West Sussex
BN6 9XU  UK      Website: www.warpoetry.co.uk

Printed and bound in Great Britain by 4Edge Ltd, 7a Eldon Way,
Eldon Way Industrial Estate, Hockley, Essex SS5 4AD  UK

**Copyright**

**Cover illustration**

Rheims Cathedral on fire after bombardment, September 1914. Contemporary
postcard. Annonymous.

**Acknowledgements**

A number of friends and colleagues have given me vital help in the preparation of
the anthology: Thierry Choffat, Humphrey Humphreys, Leo Mewse, Jérôme Nobé-
court, Paresh Raval, Peter Read, David Roberts and Nigel Wilkins. Without them,
this anthology truly could not have been what it is, and I thank them very warmly
indeed.

**Acknowledgement of Permission to Use Copyright Material**

We are grateful to the following for permission to use copyright material: Editions
Denoël – poems by Marcel Sauvage, and Nigel Wilkins – poems by Henri-Charles
Thuillier.

In spite of our best efforts it has not been possible to contact all copyright owners.
We would be pleased to hear from any copyright owners that we were unable to
trace.

# Contents

# INTRODUCTION

The British war poets of 1914–1918 have been a foundation stone of literary culture in the United Kingdom for nearly a century. The vivid classics of Owen, Rosenberg, Sassoon, Sorley and others have brought home to three generations the horror and, a persistent tradition has it, the futility of the war.

French Great War poetry, as this volume so clearly shows, is in many ways profoundly different from the best-known British poetry of the war. Yet these poets are still almost completely unknown in the United Kingdom, apart from Guillaume Apollinaire and, perhaps, Jean Cocteau.

The main reason for the differences is that, on the Western Front, the war was for the most part being fought on, and in, French soil. It was *French* soil – whether clayey or chalky – that was being poisoned, *French* villages and churches that were being left in ruins. And it was in this French soil that the very trenches were dug: many of the soldier-writers thought of themselves as being embedded in the body of France, as being part of this native earth. Apollinaire, for example, wrote of 'flowing through the war's soft sweet guts all along soft saps […] I've dug the bed I'm flowing along branching into myriad little rivers going everywhere'. The novelist and poet Lucien Rolmer wrote in a letter: 'I'm living like a root […] I feel I'm steeped in French soil. I'm giving myself.' This is a fundamentally different experience from that of the British soldier, a fact that was succinctly put by R.H. Mottram in his novel *The Spanish Farm Trilogy, 1914–1918*. A British soldier raises his hand in salute to a dead French comrade: 'I am English, he was French. He *meant* his war.' Later, this is clarified as follows: 'The English (sic) had been welcomed as Allies, resented as intruders, but never had they become homogeneous with the soil and its natives, nor could they ever leave any everlasting mark on the body or spirit of the place.' So, where Rupert Brooke could write in 'The Soldier' (1914): 'If I should die, think only this of me: / That there's some corner of a foreign field / That is for ever England', Nicolas Beauduin, in the same year, passionately addresses France thus: 'Land of my birth, my blood be seed in thee!' ('Offertory' – see page 17). This 'homogeneousness' with the soil, whereby one is both born of it and fertilises it, is a given in very much French writing of the war. The conclusion of Anna de Noailles' 'Verdun' is typical: 'Passer-by, think not to extol / The city hosts of angels shielded, sprung / From every inch of France's soil. […] / Acknowledge, in the slashed and battered plain, / The fathomless and hallowed power of France, / Whose noblest hearts now lie buried in her soil. […] / Soaked and sated, earth is made man' (see page 131).

Certainly, as well as differences, there are similarities between French poetry of the war and the British poetry we are most familiar with. Thus, in this anthology, there are many poems written in protest against the war, both by serving soldiers – Edmond Adam, Georges Chennevière, Marc de Larreguy – and by civilians – René Arcos (invalided out of the army early in the war), Pierre Jean Jouve, Marcel Martinet, Jules Romains, Henriette Sauret. Hostility to the war proceeded from a variety of standpoints: unanimist or socialist internationalism (Arcos, Chennevière, Larreguy, Romains, Martinet), a more general humanism (Sauret), or Christian (Jouve).

More prevalent, however, is an acceptance that this war *has* to be fought, in defence of what Mottram calls 'the body and spirit' of France. The invader has to be driven out, French territorial integrity restored and protected, and French culture preserved (education under the Third Republic had laid stress on the country's literary heritage in particular as constituting its true spiritual identity). So there are soldier-poets in this anthology who deplore the need to fight, and unflinchingly record the gruesome realities of the front, but who convey a dogged commitment to continuing the struggle to the end (Noël Garnier, Albert-Paul Granier, Henry-Jacques, Marc Leclerc, André Martel, François Porché). Some may seem positively enthusiastic to fight; Gabriel-Tristan Franconi is possibly one such, but Jean-Pierre Calloc'h certainly is, resolving to 'split the German's skull' – not out of bloodthirstiness, but from a passionate desire to help France rid herself of the Teutonic scourge and so, ultimately, enable his native Brittany to reclaim her own rightful identity.

Surprising as it may seem, Calloc'h is committed to this war not only as a patriot, but as an ardent Christian. So also is the civilian Paul Claudel, the best-known Catholic writer of the time in France. Henri-Charles Thuillier, a village priest, combines the Christian virtue of forgiveness with a conviction that it is France's holy duty to repel the invader. Other Christian voices are more quietist, regretting the slaughter but resigned to accepting the need for it: one such is Henriette Charasson. Charasson's resignation is in fact typical of that expressed by a number of women poets (Lucie Delarue-Mardrus, Anna de Noailles, Cécile Périn): this is a resignation that stems to a great extent from the political powerlessness of women at the time, a kind of helplessness that sometimes expresses itself as sarcastic hostility to the war (Sauret), and sometimes in indifference, an attitude deplored in various tones by Périn and Martinet. Women were not the only civilians, of course: elderly or infirm men, even though they had the vote, felt just as powerless to influence events. One such in this anthology is the author of *Cyrano de Bergerac*, Edmond Rostand, whose patriotic indignation is no less strongly felt for the elegance of its expression.

The soldiers' own attitude to civilian life, of course, grew increasingly troubled, ranging from nostalgia for home to painful awareness of the gulf of understanding between those left at home and the men at the front. This tension between tenderness and resentment underlies a number of poems in the anthology, notably by Chennevière, Garnier, Henry-Jacques and Larreguy. The relation between civilian and military life certainly changed after demobilisation, but could be just as problematic for veterans. There are poems expressing bitterness at the marginalisation of disabled soldiers – heroes yesterday, unproductive cripples today (Martinet, Sauvage). Others convey the difficulty found by even the able-bodied in readjusting to life among civilians who still cannot grasp just what it was like for the combatants (Sauvage). This resentment shades into survivor guilt, not only in soldiers (Sauvage), but even in civilians (Martinet, Noailles). War-widows, too, were faced with the challenge of how, if at all, to return to 'normality' (Périn, Sauvage).

The breadth and variety of themes and emotions in this body of poetry is matched by the range of stylistic variety. Some poets deliver themselves of orotund professions of patriotic faith. Some construct mini-epics of battlefield encounters in well-wrought traditional verse. Others avoid grandiloquence but still manage to articulate potentially inexpressible, overwhelming experience by working it into orthodox verse forms. Sometimes, these forms comprise such a jerky and extreme mixture of lengths of line that they barely register as orthodox. Some of the poets use a kind of blank verse, orthodox lines but without rhyme – very much not a French tradition. Many use free verse, as if allowing the explosive force of the events and emotions expressed to destroy prosodic convention, while improvising resourceful new ways of channelling their expression. Some write in quasi-biblical 'verses', sometimes rhetorical, sometimes almost colloquial. An extreme type of free verse is the calligram, as practised by Apollinaire, where the text is partly or wholly set in the shapes of things it refers to; there are two such poems in this selection. Jean Cocteau is almost as restless an experimenter as Apollinaire, and there are poems here by both poets marked by a registering of diverse impressions as a kind of fluid, but fragmentary, simultaneity.

Often, among the soldier-poets, there is a trench humour which combines fantasy, verbal inventiveness and a keen edge of anger. The blend makes it clear that they were not fighting simply out of a patriotic duty urged on them by eloquent civilians safe at home, but because they were vigorously proud to be facing death in defence of the people, culture and values of their mother country: the virtuoso manipulation of rhythm and rhyme leaves the reader/listener in no doubt that these men '*meant* their war'. – As did the protagonist of Marc Leclerc's extraordinary *Passion of our*

*Brother the Poilu*, translated here in its entirety: this 203-line poem comically and movingly blends dialect and everyday speech in an account of the death and transfiguration of an uneducated farmer from Anjou.

As a whole, then, the 102 poems in this anthology give a comprehensive sample of the varied, passionate and often complex attitudes of French people to the war. The poems are arranged in broadly chronological order. Many of the poets actually dated their poems. This was especially true of the soldiers, doubtless for three main reasons. First, all knew that any day could be their last: almost every day at the front, however spent, will have been lived particularly vividly. Second, each man will have been more keenly aware than in peacetime that he was actively making history, whatever he was doing – charging the enemy, manning an observation post, trying to get some sleep... Third, being poets, they will have been very conscious of making history in another way, by writing it.

Not all the poets dated their texts, however. Sometimes, the approximate date can be inferred from when the poem was published. Sometimes it can be found in correspondence or memoirs. Wherever I have been able to use such evidence, I have placed the poem accordingly. Where I have found none, I have put the poem where its subject matter or tone accords with those of neighbouring poems. Ideally, the anthology should not be dipped into, as anthologies usually are (by me at any rate), but read as if it were a single text. The result, I hope, is to give a sense of the continuous ebb and flow of moods and attitudes in France during the war and in its immediate aftermath.


## A Note on the War from a French Perspective

By 1914, the revanchism that had followed the humiliating defeat in the Franco-Prussian war of 1870–1871 was much less widespread, confined mainly to right-wing nationalists. The same period had seen a growing presence of internationalist, pacifist socialism in parliament. When mobilisation was announced on 1 August 1914, the dominant reaction was one of surprise, not bellicose enthusiasm. But when Germany declared war on 3 August, the French saw themselves as the innocent victims of aggression. The first troops to leave for the war were given the traditional heroes' send-off, with cheering crowds and girls showering them with flowers. After the German invasion later in the month, the mood changed into a resigned but firm determination to drive the invader out. Another surprise was the so-called *Union sacrée*, an ideological truce in which the opposed political groupings in France subordinated their differences to the interests of national defence.

By the end of August the German army, bigger and with superior firepower, had occupied the north-east of France and was advancing on Paris. The advance was so fast, however, that in early September the invader's flank became vulnerable to counter-attack. Gallieni, in charge of the Paris garrison, was allowed by the French Commander-in-Chief, Joffre, to make that attack. Commandeering the Paris taxicabs, he got his troops to the river Marne in time to engage the enemy. The ensuing battle of the Marne ('the miracle of the Marne') stopped the German advance. By the end of 1914 the front was static, 450 miles of trenches stretching from the Swiss border to the Channel coast.

None of the combatant armies was trained to wage trench warfare, or to cope with modern artillery and the machine-gun. Despite losing 300,000 dead before the end of 1914 (as well as the 600,000 wounded, missing or captured), the French pursued a strategy of all-out attack throughout 1915, Joffre's aim being to wear the enemy down by a war of attrition – 'je les grignote' ('I'm gnawing them away/wearing them down'), he is reported to have said. During this year, the French lost 600,000 dead, plus another 1,400,000 casualties. The *Union sacrée* showed signs of strain, some people, mainly socialists, asking whether a negotiated peace might not be better than endless bloodletting.

1916 saw the battle that more than any other encapsulates the Great War for French people: Verdun. Verdun was a fortress city of great historical and symbolic significance, although in 1916 the city itself had little military importance. Nevertheless, there were half a million French troops in the area. Verdun was defended by a system of outlying forts, notably Vaux and Douaumont. The Germans reasoned that French morale would not survive its loss; indeed, Erich von Falkenhayn, the German chief of general staff, claimed after the war that the strategy had been a prolonged assault which would 'bleed France white'.

Whether or not this really was the plan at the outset, the battle did turn out to be one of attrition. On 21 February, the Germans launched the greatest artillery bombardment yet seen. Over the next few days they advanced three miles. Fort Douaumont fell on the 25th. (Fort Vaux held out until June.) Suffering huge losses, the French duly poured reserves in to replace them. The men and munitions were transported from Bar-le-Duc along a road that came to be known as *la Voie Sacrée* (the Holy Way). Under General Pétain, the French showed incredible courage and obstinacy as the slaughter continued, with minimal advances and retreats, all through the summer. Fort Douaumont was retaken on 24 October, Fort Vaux on 3 November. The struggle for Verdun itself can be reckoned to have been over by the end of July, but the battle went on until December. Verdun itself never fell, and, from 21 February to 31 December, the Germans suffered very nearly as many casualties (roughly 337,000) as the French (roughly 377,000). During the battle, three-quarters of the French army were involved in the battle at one point or another. It should not be forgotten, of course, that 1916 was also the year of the Somme (July–November). The French suffered 190,000 casualties in that battle, a loss rate actually higher than at Verdun. But while other battles claimed more lives, the Verdun battlefield saw more dead per square metre than any. Small wonder, then, that Verdun has even greater significance for the French than the Somme has for the British, carrying an almost sacred memory of, and gratitude for, the self-sacrifice of the 162,440 Frenchmen killed in the battle.

By the end of 1916, militaristic enthusiasm for the war had all but evaporated in France. Civilians had already felt the increase in the cost of living in 1915. Things grew dearer still in 1916, and price controls were introduced. (Shortages of fuel and food were to become more serious in 1917, and rationing was introduced in 1918.) At the end of 1916, Joffre was replaced as Commander-in-Chief by General Nivelle. Despite the carnage at Verdun, civilian morale still held more or less firm, thanks partly to the strict censorship imposed throughout the war and partly to a largely gung-ho press. Most soldiers called this triumphalist propaganda *bourrage de crâne* – not, strictly speaking, 'brainwashing', more 'stuffing heads with rubbish'. They were angered by the disparity between the realities of the front and the rosy picture painted of it for civilian consumption. It was hard enough for a soldier on leave to put his experiences into words. When civilians then either could or would not hear the truths they were being told, he felt estranged from his fellow-citizens. (Conversely, of course, he would often consciously conceal the horrors, in order to reassure his loved ones.) The best-known exponent of *bourrage de crâne* was the nationalist novelist Maurice Barrès, who wrote a regular column throughout the war in the *Écho de Paris*. It was Barrès who coined the name *Voie Sacrée*. Most soldiers despised him as a hypocritical armchair warmonger. Others revered in him the most eloquent advocate of a notion of *patrie* as a soil nourished by the nation's dead and made sacred by their blood; indeed, Nicolas Beauduin and François Porché , both featured in this anthology, fulsomely dedicated works to him.

From the end of 1916, the population as a whole took *bourrage de crâne* less and less seriously. The first half of 1917 saw a genuine faltering in the morale of civilians and soldiers alike. This was due primarily to the expensive failure of suicidal attacks repeatedly launched by Nivelle in April at the Chemin des Dames, a ridge between the river Aisne and Laon. The pointlessness of this massacre led to Nivelle's replacement, on 15 May, by Pétain. Pétain's first job was to deal with an outbreak of mutinies, which he did with firmness and a sensitivity that further enhanced the reputation of 'the saviour of Verdun'. This temporary crisis in army morale was paralleled by growing criticism in some newspapers of the conduct of the war. In addition, socialist internationalism began to reassert itself more strongly and, inasmuch as the socialists withdrew from government, the *Union sacrée* was less of a reality. There were a number of strikes in May and June, some of them in munitions factories. These were motivated mainly by anxiety about rising prices, although anti-war slogans were sometimes heard. However, military morale seems to have recovered in the second half of 1917. The predominant view among the population as a whole was that, after such enormous sacrifices, nothing less than total victory would do.

In December 1917, revolutionary Russia signed an armistice with Germany, which could now concentrate its forces in the west. In March, the Germans launched a major offensive. Between then and June they drove the Allies back along the whole of the front, coming back to the Marne forty miles from Paris. Paris itself, which had suffered air raids since 1915, came under fire from huge guns. The situation was grave. General Foch was appointed supreme commander of the allied armies, which now included United States forces. In July, Foch counter-attacked, and the Germans were steadily driven back. Finally, they agreed to an armistice, signed on 11 November 1918.

France had lost 1,322,000 men killed in the Great War, a higher proportion of those mobilised than for Britain, Germany or Russia. In 1919, French agriculture and industry produced little more than half what they had in 1913.

# Offertory

I offer thee the life thou gavest me,
I offer thee my flesh that thou didst mould,
I offer thee, my Country, my ardent soul;
Land of my birth, my blood be seed in thee!

May this, my body's fervent last oblation,
When this my sacrifice has fully bled,
Be pleasing to you Powers of salvation,
Who guide the living and protect the dead.

                              NICOLAS BEAUDUIN


# Orison

Supreme, the hour of suffering draws near.
That thou, my country, stand great again and free,
Do we solemn, willing victims here
Offer, France, our holocaust to thee.

At this blood-red breaking of the Dawn,
Give us, Lord, the power to conquer pain,
And strength, the thirst for suffering to sustain –
And soon to die, that others might live on.

Grant our dearest hopes their full fruition:
In us the miracle of paradise
Be wrought, through our pious sacrifice,
And every sinning soul saved from perdition!

                              NICOLAS BEAUDUIN

# To Norman Lads

Splendid hedges, splendid beasts;
The fields and blossom of dreams;
The sky a coloured, mirrored feast
Bubbling down the stream

Through perfect pasture to the sea;
Hay ready for the manger –
Such is our country: keep her free,
Our country is in danger!

Do you own, or simply work, the land?
– Arise and hurry! Now!
Stout of heart and firm of hand,
Save the fields you plough.

The foe might come by sea, to this shore;
By land, or from the skies.
Listen how your stallion cries!
To war, you must to war.

Norman lads have eyes of blue,
Let them glint and pierce.
March cheerful, though the guns be fierce,
Battalions bold and true.

Away to fight, my warrior kin,
Take the road to fame.
Tomorrow's history shall begin
With your impatient name.

Our country bids you leave your corn,
The harvest still not done!
But flowers from your fields adorn
The muzzles of your guns.

Make haste! Sing as you depart,
And you arm for carnival;
March with poems in your heart,
And war is festival.

A great tragedy is about to play.
Leave no thing to chance:
Arise, my Normandy, away
And save the soil of France!

LUCIE DELARUE-MARDRUS

# Hate

O gentle fellow dreamers,
how fondly you charm the dreams,
how skilfully ride the will o' the wisp;
how your peaceable, heroic souls
thrill to breathe among the galaxies...
– O you devoted lovers of the stars, we have now
to turn our backs on that spellbinding sight
of dreams dancing shimmering into magic flight,
the roomfuls of calm and well-wishing,
the still inwardness of reflections in their mirrors,
the ministering lamp's caress of gold...
Ah, those soft, silent, lampglow evenings
coaxing the play of sheen and sparkle,
like a woman looking at jewels,
from the gleam of verse white-cushioned in its book;
the fevered nights, drunk on thought,
intent over poems
as gem-cutters over stones...

– All that! We have to leave it all behind!
We, the nectar-gatherers of the mind, have now
to grasp the old, long-wearied longbow of the will,
and flex and tense it
and let fly Hatred, stinging shafts of Hate!

Hate! Hate! How the word hurts!
Hate, we have to hate;
Hatred unto ecstasy.

ALBERT-PAUL GRANIER
1914

## Burning Beehives

How pleasing: straight away, they burned some beehives…

O bees, tumbling, buzzing gold in the blue air,
As long as you're aloft they haven't triumphed,
O last little glimmer from the golden age!

'But why ever are you burning my bees?'
The curé of Fraimbois asked the German brute.
'That's war!' replied the General. – Yes, war as waged
By the horde on the buzz and pride of freedom.
Why, then, did they burn this hive of straw?
Because the hive at work intoned a psalm
As it fashioned what resembled sunbeams.
And earlier, remember, on entering Brussels,
The Chiefs had issued orders to their thugs
To trample the flowerbeds underfoot.

As janissaries rush to please their vizier,
So the soldiers joyed to stamp down the flowers.
That they should blithely now be burning beehives
Is simple logic: it is but one short step,
One goose-step, from trampled flowers to bees in flames.
How they flared and crackled in the blue air,
And dropped! A fine sight; and the perfumed wax
Streaming black! And then, burn a beehive,
And up in smoke go famous names as well –
Plato, Vergil, La Fontaine, Maeterlinck –
Alongside the bees, as if to fade away,
A further fading out of humanism
To mark the triumph of the feldgrau lout.

The bee is spirit visible in light,
A drop of honey risen on two wings!
How might it ever find forgiveness from
Such clods? The bee is instant choice, sureness
Of touch and taste: briefly floating, exploring –
Then aim, effort, balance, judgement, skill!
And when the human mind in wonderment
Sees, deep in a hive, its own destiny
Mysteriously sketched out by pure instinct,
To serve the Hun it is disinclined! – Rather
This sweet, free order than their Discipline!
Yes, hives murmur. – All murmuring will
At once be shriven, purged and burnt alive!
No bee ever weighed heavy on a rose,
Or cumbersomely hoarded: bees compose,
Benignly reasoning that under heaven
None should sting, save in defence of honey;
The bee discommodes the barbarous – they hate,
As much as they despise, this citizen
Who fortifies with simple fragile bud glue
A city built from the sap of lilies!
These golden fliers' blond straw huts needs must burn,

That there remain henceforth but iron wasps
In nests of concrete over all the world!
Their wish – if wish it be – is that nevermore
In any man any dream be dreamed,
Nor in any garden any hive be found,
That sheer grinding matter wear us down!
Once conquered, you would see, in your suddenly
Useless trellises and roses, not
One single bee! And by 'not one single bee'
I mean no remaining trace of harmony,
Nothing noble, pure, light as air –
None of what sustains a Latin's heart!
No refuge anywhere, not even a book –
For jackboots trampling roses stamp on Ronsard,
And should we chance to open a Chénier
Burnt bees would drop from between the leaves!

Sweet fruit of time, dark-treasured honey, stored
Humble in Fraimbois, grander in Louvain…
No more beehives, no more future, no broods
Fed in secret from the flowers of vines!
'But why,' the poor priest asked, 'why burn my beehives?'
Pleasing, then, that to the bees' good shepherd
The Burner of bees said 'That's war'. –Their war, yes,
But what of ours?

                    In those first, tragic days,
When our troops were moving north to Belgium,
It is told that French armoured cavalry
Rode through a Flemish village – I forget
The name – their horses festooned with roses,
Singing, as they rode, the Marseillaise –
But through their teeth, mouths closed, simply humming;
And it was magnificent. And this hum
Of Latin anger from across all those flowers,
Wordless, and gestureless, was the growl

Of mind and soul, it was conscience, and reason;
The sound of storm and oratory, pious,
Threatening, and with a fierce, golden
Calm. Not a single mouth was seen to move,
As though it were the flowers themselves that hummed.
And those who heard it, eyes filled with tears, thought
To hear, in the reddening evening dust,
Some kind of strange Marseillaise hummed by bees…
Thus, with purity and purpose, did our men
Transmute their warlike anthem into a swarm's hum,
As north they rode, prepared for ambush, prepared to die
For beehives and to save the honey of the world!

EDMOND ROSTAND


## Force of Habit

Speaking to the village priest,
A German captain, furious:
There is fury in his voice,
With its harsh, emphatic beat,
There is fury in his face –
'You are lyink,' he repeats.

'Dere vos a shot, a shot from here,
From der tower of der church.'
'Perhaps you ought to start a search,'
Replies the priest, his conscience clear,
'But let me fetch a lantern first,
And guide your way, for night is near.'

'I say again: dere vos a shot,
As if der church vos a retoubt.
You vos der shniper, dere's no toubt:
Are you der shniper?' 'I am not.'
'Com outsite, just com out,
I proof it, I show you der shpot.'

The priest follows him outside,
Firm of step, undismayed.
Hearing him begin to pray,
The imperious German shouts:
'You vill be shot, shtraight avay –
Shtand here, against dis fountain.'

Just then – where from, no one knows,
But with a roar like rushing waters –
Next to where the two are talking
An enormous bomb explodes.
Instantly, the German falls;
The priest absolves him, that he be whole.

But the German was too dead,
The unscathed priest's concern too late.
They said: 'Don't pity him his fate –
You're too forgiving… you're misled…'
'My strength is to forgive, not to hate,
I'm used to it,' the good priest said.

HENRI-CHARLES THUILLIER

# The Shrapnel-Burst

'Do your duty, Priest, and I'll do mine.'
'Who's that?'
           'It's me.'
                  'But you're not a Christian –
You told me once, and aimed your rifle at me.'
'I do admit, I was no friend of priests.
I'd been fed such curé-hating rubbish!
My paper called them hideous hypocrites,
Spongers, tyrants, the vampires of our day.
"However black they're painted," my friends maintained,
"They're even blacker." But I know better now.
I know they're good French citizens; and I've found
That they are men of true sincerity.
I trust more now in all their rituals.
My mother told me, at the start, "Remember!"
I did remember; I've felt the faith come back.
The fault was mine, I ask for God's forgiveness:
I want my fault washed out. So get up, Priest!
Give me the pardon of your God – *my* God,
And I'll be even stronger under fire.'
The Priest stood up, and said, 'Your penitence
Shall be to hold firm in resistance here,
Like me, to the last.'
                  'Yes, that's *it* – like you!'
The Priest continues, 'Ego te absolvo.'
His comrade crosses himself, head lowered,
And both go back to their respective posts…
…But no, their souls are both with God eternal.
They died together in one burst of shrapnel.

HENRI-CHARLES THUILLIER

# The Vandal's Death

A shell has burst at the abandoned altar
And splashed rosace blood from porch to crypt;
The martyred country church lies bullet-whipped,
Offering her body in holy dignity
To a brutish, wine-excited soldiery;
And in the village, cock-crow's heard no more.

A frightened savage, far from those he loves,
Dies at the forced door of the church, in prayer
To the god of love whose hearth he defiled;
In the apse, shells have whizzed and flared.
The Teuton's blue eyes have died to the light,
But the steeple cock still proudly crows above.

GABRIEL-TRISTAN FRANCONI

# Squall

A steel squall of gluttonous thrusting shells smashed
thunderclaps through clear sky
straight at the village, ferocious
as a swoop of eagles on a flock of grazing sheep.

And when the bloated eddies of smoke had rolled away
across the quiet pastureland,
the peaceful village by its river
was gone, and in its place was only ruin, desolation.
The church, amongst the dead of years past, is doomed,
but just still standing, like a dying horse, its very soul
bleeding from the riven stones,

weeping from every dead louvre in the lurching belfry
that it cannot sound this night a pious death-knell
for the peaceful village by the river.

ALBERT-PAUL GRANIER<br>1914

# When it's Us 'Who Were in the War'

I never shall forget Vareddes
The day after the battle:
The trees, those great gashes;
The dead horses, those rigid legs;

The musky, cloying smell of gangrene
Slinking through the village;
And, behind a grille,
A lean dog with hyena eyes.

A cottage, its doorway wrecked,
Was humming like a hive
From round a wingback chair
The peasant woman sat in, dead.

Scattered helmets, bottles, packs
And a pianola –
Weird heroic tokens
Of yesterday's momentous action.

Can Vareddes ever resurrect
And be what it was before,
When it's us who were In the War,
Our youth long since laid to rest?

When you wish the day could dawn,
With the journey still before you,
And you were being told the stories,
And not the one who tells them.

JEAN COCTEAU

# Exodus

*To Émile Verhaeren*

Away along the claggy tracks
leading in from the plains,
the people are leaving, gone mad perhaps,
gone wisely mad perhaps,
the people are going – away, anywhere but here…

Into long carts done out with hay
they've loaded their worldly wealth:
their Sunday best,
mattresses, white blankets,
the photographs of the boys
away in the war,
and the grandmother's bridal spray
in its glass dome,
                              and they go away,
leaving Christ above the hearth,
that His supplicating arms might turn aside
the brutal, looting rampage of an army.

An aged horse, gaunt on poverty,
led by a child,
hauls a trap, panting,
with women and an old man
following on foot, not to weary further
the broken-down old horse's weary tramp –
following the trap
like the hearse of their past,
following in resignation,

dragging their cattle,
those neat pointed feet and gentle eyes…
The people are leaving, people
who long were mad perhaps,
and staring now
at visions only they can see:
memories perhaps, or hopes…

From village to village,
wordless, starving, pinched,
away the people drag, on and on,
– some dropping where they trudge, dead meat already –,
their only future – when not death –
the fields in flames and the farm looted,

– away, to bury their hate like dead cattle,
bunch their knuckles to their eyes,
slump down and weep on a heap of stones,
choke weeping…

Away along the claggy tracks
leading in from the plains,
the people are leaving, gone mad perhaps…

ALBERT-PAUL GRANIER
Les Éparges 1914

# The Cathedral

They have but left it somewhat more immortal.
Laid waste by oafish mischief, Great Works do not perish.
Ask Phidias, ask Rodin: there is more to cherish
In the fragments, familiar, eternal.

A fortress dismantled truly dies:
The shattered Temple lives nobler, and one disdains
To regret that so little of the roof remains:
The sky through the lace of stone delights the eye.

Let us thank – for we were lacking still
What the Greeks have on their golden hill,
Beauty's Symbol sanctified by slight –

Thank the skilled aimer of the numbskull gun
For this fruit of German martial might:
Deep Shame for them; for us, a Parthenon!

EDMOND ROSTAND

# The Cathedral

Guns, old comrades!
old slumberers suddenly roused
from long, deep fortress-sleep,
ancestral steel black-muscle-bound,
heavy veterans, barrel-jawed,
connoisseurs of cordite,
steel-eaters, fire-smokers,
proud, full-throated singers –
sing out the lovely wedding hymn
of pale mankind and death!
Sing it! Sing! Sing again!
let the echo thunder from inside
every resounding cloud
to repeat the mighty funeral chorus,
the fearsome, red-lightning-candled
wedding march.

Growl, my old friends, clamour, turn
and massacre, annihilate!
They have assassinated the Cathedral!
– smashed the high doors down,
smashed the stately legends
of the saints tall in their stained glass,
and the golden light and purple shade
of the prodigious rose window,
that symbolic radiant monstrance
illuminating an ecstatic world!

They've blasted the high arches in,
smashed down the colonnades of pinnacles
that hungered for the sky,
they've slashed to shreds the lacework of stone,
they've killed the silence that had forever slept
under solemn vaulting . . .

O guns, good guns, my old friends!
over all the endless plains
clamour forth the universal pain!
The Cathedral that transcends humanity
is dying; howl death,
like roaming dogs in moonlight,
shout! roar! Louder, ever louder!
roar open-jawed, roar my hatred at them!
Avenge the gentle stained-glass saints
who for centuries shone down
in stately absolution,
avenge the unwinged angels
and the grey lead gargoyles
smelted in the flames!

They have assassinated the Cathedral!

O guns, good guns, my guns,
my poor voice is shouted hoarse!
shout for me, roar for me
your most colossal execration,
hurl my anathema, my curses,
cry vengeance! cry vengeance!
and I shall feed you all the lovely cordite
and heavy steel that you can swallow!
rear and stamp, like maddened horses!
spew cataracts of hate on them!
Roar! roar! even unto death!
and roar your dying gasp!
O guns, good guns, my friends!
they have murdered memory!
they have
assassinated the Cathedral!

ALBERT-PAUL GRANIER
1914

# The Bleeding-Heart Dove and the Fountain

Gentle faces stabbed and bleeding Sweetheart lips in bloom
MIA                                    MAREYE
YETTE                                LOREYE
ANNIE        and you        MARIE
where                            are
you                O
sweet   girls
BUT
above
a praying
weeping fountain
hovers this ecstatic dove

These memories are all so recent
O you my friends marched off to war
Welling and hurling heavenwards
Your eyes' light drowsing in the water
Sorrowfully fading dying
Where are Braque and Max Jacob
Derain with those dawn-grey eyes

?

Where are Dalize Billy Raynal
Their names diffusing into sorrow
Like sombre footfalls in a church
Cremnitz volunteered where is he
All already dead perhaps
Memories brimming in my heart
The fountain weeping to my pain

THOSE STATIONED IN THE NORTH ARE IN THE FRONT LINE FIGHTING NOW

Evening falls O sea of blood

Warrior oleander blossom bleeding wreathes the garden walls

GUILLAUME APOLLINAIRE

# Under the Yoke

The country is a burning
Furnace searing brows and hearts;
Bitter grief, unease and fear
Spreading everywhere.

Gripped by legal stricture,
Minds forced down onto the anvil:
Recant, repent, ye free of spirit!
And art fading in the fog.

The slightest flight of fancy –
Quiet! There is this heavy Something,
This oppressive imposition,
Smothering expression.

Nothing is exempt,
Not one clear spring or oasis;
All the peoples struggling, breathless,
Sucked down into the mess.

The proudest races now
Are but purveyors of carrion,
The continent of Enlightenment
But a slaughterhouse.

This waking nightmare hounds me,
That men are still no further forward
Than the basest instincts warped:
The brawl, the chase, the kill.

Oh, to flee this worst of prisons,
Where souls breathe their damnation;
To flee anathema and cannon…
Oh, desert islands, distant oceans…

HENRIETTE SAURET
September 1914

35

# War Song

Dame Death is joyously dancing,
a drunken, hip-swinging jig,
never a word, just wriggling
and playfully juggling skulls
like so many knucklebones.

Dame Death is glad, and very drunk –
for there's blood in full flow out there,
a heavy red brookful in every ravine.

Accompanying her weird dancing
is the tom-tom of guns in the distance:
'Tom-tom-tom! tom-tom-tom! Come then, White Lady,
come dance to the sound of the drums!'

Dame Death's getting drunker and splashing
her sweet little face with blood,
like a child who's been eating the jam.

Dame Death is paddling in blood,
and slapping down into it with her long hands,
as though she were washing her shroud;
wallowing, and silently sniggering.
Dame Death is flushed, writhing, dancing
like a girl who's had too much drink.

'Hey, Death, get your hopping in time
with the tom-tom of guns in the distance!'

– Tomtomtom-tomtomtom!

The guns in the distance
quicken their murderous presto,
guns laughing together in rhythm;
the guns in the band force the tempo,
whipping her up for the Jubilation Ball:

'Spin on those dainty slim feet,
squirm the meat off those sinuous hips,
get waltzing and whirling, White Lady!
dancing and skipping! waving your arms!
Here's blood, here's blood!
And here's some more, to keep you going!
Come on now, drink up! totter and reel!
This is the start of the Orgy in Red!'

Dame Death is dancing, insanely drunk,
to the tom-tom of guns in the distance.

ALBERT-PAUL GRANIER
1914

# For my Immeasurable Love

For my immeasurable love,
Which no heroism, nor any reason of State,
Nor any witness borne to human wickedness,
Nor any of the truths powerfully woken by war,
Can constrain to admit defeat,
For my immeasurable love, I want nothing
Save the right to be one among many immeasurables.
I stand here in the depth of the life of war,
A solitary lover of a life of peace,
A life of relations built of peace,
Happiness, prior agreement,
And fellowship with that Work whose goal is unknown,
But which demands all our might, until our very death –
No need for treaties to establish such a peace,
We shall be agreed as we set to work,
As we agree over a beautiful day or a blade of grass.

And, my soul brimful of such future, with scarce a thought for the
    present,
I await the advent of an imperishable love.

PIERRE JEAN JOUVE
November 1914

# God With Us

*Emmanuel, which, being interpreted, is, God with us.*
Matthew 1 : 23

Their *Gott mit Uns* to all four winds they yell.
God with *them*? Such is their fondest dream.
But in the cry our forebears loved, *Nowell*,
Do we not hear ring out the self-same theme?

While their word *Gott* sounds a harsher knell,
Like Odin, cruel god, a dismal scream,
Our *Nowell* evokes the heavenly smell
Of a newly-dawned, rose-scented sunbeam.

No! God is not quite banished from our land:
In our age-old words He's still at hand.
The French did stray… but *French* preserved the law!

Friends, take up the old triumphant cry:
Let us sing *Nowell* to God once more,
For He's with us, not them – the Lord on high!

HENRI-CHARLES THUILLIER
Neuve-Lyre, 25 December 1914

# Veni, Sancte Spiritus!

*A Song of welcome to the New Year*

## I

Now in the one thousand nine hundred and fourteenth year after
    Christ was born in the stable;
Like the Poor man's face all at once against the windows of the
    worldly rich at their wild dancing;
Like the three words on the wall, when Belshazzar made his
    great feast;
Like a moon of grief and terror, blinding each day's sun with its
    savage splendour,
Over every contemptible horizon of the Strumpet Europe,
    The blood-face of War!
And before that terrible Star every star fell back, cast into the depths
    of night;
And all works ceased, until the Great Work should be wrought;
And men fixed their eyes upon fields of carnage, the place of
    celebration of a great Mystery, a transcendental Sacrifice,
The Mass whose celebrant is Fire, its unexampled music the gun,
    the Mass whose victim they call the son of man.

## II

Like those who sing the Good News through all Brittany, from door
    to door, at the blessed feast of Christmas,
(In commemoration of the angels who proclaimed peace to all men in
    that first night of Christianity),
I have sought my brothers tonight, to give them greetings from
    the bard,
And found no one in their homes…
The gentle homes of Celts are empty, save for some, here and there,
    where the fire died long ago,
And by the dead fire poor women weep, and little children dream,
    and dream…

O my Lord God, what plague has passed over this land?

Where are you, Celt of mountain Scotland? And you, Celt of Ireland?
Celt of Wales, where are you? And you, my own blood, Celt of
Brittany, where are you?

Empty, the gentle homes of Celts! As the summer sun rose over the
valley, the men left, taking their swords...

### III

Once, they carried lances; now they have rifles.

Rifles and cannon spewing death, but a sword is still a sword,

And the ages have wrought no change in the accursed German heart.

Who shall resist the endless westward German surge, if the Celt does
not rise against the German now?

The Celt has done as his fathers did: with song on his lips, he has
marched.

Wherefore raise a cheer! For Celts are still Celts: our young men are
at the frontier.

Fall upon the German, beloved brethren! The lands you defend
are your lands.

The West is ours. The West belongs to us. If the German would defile
the West, then we shall split the German's skull.

We have defended the West against every horde.

The marchlands of Gaul are a graveyard to Barbarians; our soil is rich
with their corpses.

The Barbarian today is once again the German! Fall upon the German,
since he would have it so!

Fall upon the Burner of churches, the one who burned the Wonder
of Rheims,

Church of anointed kings, where it was so sweet to pray beneath the
wing of French glories.

Forward, good Celt! and shoot, and thrust and strike! Fall if you fall:
it is for our country! But thrust and strike, thrust and strike,
O my brother, thrust and strike!

Without rest, without cease, without mercy, thrust and strike! Kill and strangle, since you must! O my brother, kill!

Be the flail to thrash, the rock to crush, the lightning to blast, the sea
to drown:

Be the Warrior!

Remember the matchless deeds of your fathers, remember that
the German trembled beneath the gaze of their eyes.

Remember that you bear the honour of your Race: if you return,
return a conqueror!

The bard will make brave songs for the brave, Celtic songs to stir the
bones of the ancients in the cold of their graves!

## IV

I sleep no more. There is a voice, in the winter night, calling to me,
a strange voice;

A strong voice, and harsh, a voice accustomed to command: such
a voice rings agreeably in young men's ears;

(And it is no woman's voice, nor that mermaid voice that haunts
the Celtic sea);

A voice that none can disobey: War, howling at the frontiers.

I will obey. Soon I shall be with my brothers, a soldier following
soldiers.

Soon I shall be among the slaughter… What signs are on my brow?
New year, shall I see your end?

But it is of no account! Sooner, or later, when the hour to approach
the Father sounds, I shall go with gladness. Jesus shall comfort
our mothers.

Be blessed, new year, even should, among your three hundred and
sixty-five days, there be my last!

Be blessed! For more than one hundred years have passed over this
land and known only the anger of God, but you shall witness
His mercies.

You shall see banished beliefs return, the wings of victory spread
again, under the beating flag of France, and our country exalted
for evermore;

You shall see my Brittany free at last, and her language held in honour,
  as it was when her knights were alive to defend her.

New year, year of war! Be blessed, even should you bring, wrapped
  in the folds of your cloak, next to springtime for the world,
  death for me.

What is the death of one man, or one hundred, the death of one
  hundred thousand men, if our country only live, if the race
  still live...

When I die, say the prayers and bury me like my fathers, my face
  set towards the enemy,

And ask nothing for me of my Redeemer, except the last place in
  His Paradise...

V

I see, I see

God's scourge across the shoulders of Humanity. The earth and
  the seas are red with blood.

Blood over the west, blood over the north; blood in the south and
  the east: here is penitence indeed!

Now weigh your sinfulness, Europe, by the hell-glow of the fires:
  you spat in the face of my Christ on His cross, and now the hour
  of Reckoning has struck.

The hour of carnage and terror; the hour of thunder and lightning
  and tears; the hour of God's judgement!

They shall have their fill this year, the wolf, the crow and the worm:
  Christian flesh is cheap!

This year's corn will be good: the earth has drunk of human blood...

Ah, Europe! had you but wished it, this fate would not have
  been yours;

Had you but respectfully and gladly drunk His Blood, you would not
  now be choking on the blood of ten nations;

Had you but gladly and adoringly knelt before the body of God on
  Calvary, you would not now, Europe, O Europe, be so filled
  with bodies...

Grief, grief! The bells of the Earth toll only for deaths now: I see the souls of dead warriors across the battlefield like spindrift over a sea...

## VI

A plain. Bodies on the plain, thousands and more thousands. And standing among the bodies, like Ezekiel in his exile once, the poor bard calls out to you, Spirit.

Come, Holy Spirit!

Your coming is prophesied by One who spoke no falsehood, by Him who bore His suffering alone, and died denied, between the unbending branches of a cross.

Come, Holy Spirit!

And today, yes! still today! there are those who weep for You in the darkness, in a world which has lost its God.

Come, Holy Spirit!

Oh! we ask not to contemplate Your glory in its noon, but only, as God granted Moses to glimpse the Promised Land, to glimpse from afar, for one hour, the face of a world made new by You, and then to die.

Come, Holy Spirit!

For shall it never be given to us to build hearth and home on the foundation of Your peace? Shall it always be vain, our building of houses and cities, shall the breath of War always blast them?

Come, Holy Spirit!

How shall we live, if not made strong by You. Old is the son of man, and cold the earth under his poor body.

Come, Holy Spirit!

Father of the Poor, Light of our hearts! Comforter, O most excellent Comforter, in the misery of this war, whose like men have never seen, we beseech You: come to us with the new year!

## VII

I know that You will come. I know that You are near. I believe in the mystery of Grief.

'There is no birth without pain' is life's teaching to the bard. And the
    bard's to life: 'No pain without a birth. There is no sorrow that is
    barren, for such is the Law;
And has been, since Sorrow found a wedded Husband, Him whom
    the centuries have crucified, and crucified.'
The seed must die if it is to spring up and thrive. I see the bodies of
    my brothers like seeds in the earth: on their ashes wonderful fruit
    shall thrive...
Like a barbarian king who wraps himself in crimson before lying
    down to die, the year's last sun has sunk in a shroud of blood...
Tomorrow the sun shall shine upon the World!
And, like the woman in labour when she sees the face of the child
    born to her, when it sees the beauty of the new Day the Earth
    shall not remember its pain.

JEAN-PIERRE CALLOC'H
Paris, January 1915

# The Volunteers

Iron-clad in ice, the road
is scrabbled at and gripped by shod hooves
as the cart slowly lumbers away,
sprouting soldiers and tangles of waving arms:
the cart setting off, who knows where to…
off somewhere, at a slow walk,
who knows what for…

tousled with shouts and laughter.

The cart is fizzing with intensity,
whirling all its voices into clouds
as it lumbers away, dishevelled with sounds
like a railway train mushroomed with smoke.

The voices swirl and settle
on those left behind, standing at the roadside;
the voices fade away, like the pink steam
round huddles of tidy trackside shrubs
along the platform in country stations
when there's no noise from the trains…

The cart, glittering with glints of metal,
swarming with tingles of energy and hope,
rumbles calmly on, towards victory,
or disaster and rout,
to the slow, hard tread of its eight horses.

ALBERT-PAUL GRANIER
January 1915

# Regiments

All these boys who have left,
These soldiers reared to abominate war,
    Were little babies once, held
Snug and swaddled in a mother's arms.

All a-swagger in steel helmets,
They march towards the crack of flung lightning,
    And leave behind that other hell,
The sorry female hell of tears and silence.

Mothers, in your inmost being, deep
Flesh of your flesh, you carried your children;
    For you, victory and defeat
Are one: you hold your children's deaths a crime.

But I just watch these lads march away,
And think in stupefaction of their birth;
    And deep inside myself I say:
'All these men's heads have torn women with pain.'

LUCIE DELARUE-MARDRUS

## 'Eighteen, and singing songs...'

Eighteen, and singing songs, your sons, your lovely
Boys, the adventurers in love with glory,
Have left. So pure the passion in them burned,
So sovereign, that you looked on without a word,

Dissent dying on your timid lips,
So awestruck were we all at so much hope,
For these, so lately children, so very soon
To be our masters, would have mocked our protests.

O youth of France, sublime in your excitement,
Marching to death, you have never known life,
Headlong into night or to the heights,
Refusing to admit your sacrifice.

CÉCILE PÉRIN

# Perhaps the End is Still Far Distant...

Perhaps the end is still far distant,
Sisters (for this has made us sisters):
We must wait.
Do not listen, in the quiet of night, to what sound like moans:
It is only the wind blowing and the rattle of the rain,
It is not Them calling to us, do not listen to this fear in our hearts.
Sisters, we must wait, since our country asks it of us;
Let us, in silence, remain in our homes.
Perhaps our happiness weighs little at this time in the great balance
     of humanity;
Let us clamp our teeth on our sorrow, and watch the scales tilting.
We count for nothing in the future of France.
O my country, take my tears if you need them;
Take those we love, pound their flesh in the terrible mortar,
Leave our lives desolate until our time comes to die.
It is for you, our France, for you, who for us are like a living person,
For you who do truly live, shaped by the aspirations of our hearts.

Soon, I shall be no more, and my unhappiness and my happiness, and my
     wish for joy, and all the sickness of my poor burned-out heart
Will be no more, in my France's past, than another grain of sand under
     the rolling, rising, falling, heavy majesty of the transparent sea.
But this desperate subjugation of my need for happiness,
My irritated 'Hush' to the paltry self-centredness of human beings –
Surely, O my country, these things are not of no use to our national soul?
Other women who have remained at home, war by war, have bowed their
     heads
And accepted what was needed for you to shine your light over times
     to come.

O my country, who through so many centuries have been given life
    by all our dead,
O my country, who were always fed and watered, who still today
    are fed and watered,
By the purest of your blood, the noblest of your youth,
Strike them down if you must: we shall weep, but we shall murmur
    no complaint.


Yet life was beautiful in that beautiful, fresh new summer:
We had hold of all of life, we thought we could mould it as we pleased,
We too readily forgot the mysterious purpose of our lives,
And that we are not on earth to seek mere happiness.
Now we see that where we thought we were running free,
    we were marking time in a ditch,
And it was your mighty clarion voice, War, that called us from the ditch –
And They went, away down the white road, for they understood why
God had called them in those very days.
And we, poor women, we are here, waiting for the great voice
    to be still,
And only by kneeling, in silence, can we prove our love to our country.
Perhaps the end is still far distant,
Sisters; we must wait...
Let us not hurry Destiny, let us remain at prayer,
Let not the country, as it bleeds, hear our voices raised.
If the humblest of us carries in her heart a subtle strength,
If our bruised love is one more soldier in the mystery of combat,
Oh, then let us dedicate ourselves to the Country and give up to it
    what we hold dearest!
Women are given no role on the battlefield;
Here is all we have to give:
Our peacefulness, our love, and this intoxicating certainty that we
    are not alone,
And this need to be protected, and, strongest and sweetest of all,
The motherly joy of serving those we love.

But we are nothing in all of Time's continuance,
And France exists, France *is*, for ever, and shall be the more
    beautiful if we are beautiful!
Let not our weeping be too loud; let not the country, as it bleeds,
    hear our voices raised,
Sisters, we must wait:
Perhaps the end is still far distant.

HENRIETTE CHARASSON
January 1915

# To my Son

My child, you were not old enough for war,
Not required to respond to the call.
The day you were born – yesterday! – fate
And your unwitting mother saved your life.
Just three years older, and a child can die –
For children still they are, all those boys, sublime
In their dying, like flames on the skyline,
While your sweet life is still lived here, with me,
And the clock sounds dainty, suffocating chimes
As you recite your homework for tonight.
– And now see how easily a new year starts!
My heart grows less accustomed by the day
To the mysterious, blood-drenched lunacy –
And that is what I think of with racing heart
As you sit absorbed in French History,
Your hand resting on the desk – an ordinary,
Humble hand, never having killed.

ANNA DE NOAILLES
January 1915

# Horizon Blue

Farewell, proud scarlet! We must yield to reason,
And have our men go into battle less exposed.
But only the horizon is fit to clothe our heroes –
You, who are the Future's garrison.

Defending the Future in blue horizon:
A noble uniform for a noble mission.
This blue is a sign; and by this sign you shall vanquish
Their muddy grey that mimics fort and prison.

Since they have chosen the drab of earth and dust,
I think it salutary, right and just
That France and clear sky be seen as one blue morning;

And it is fitting, for the whole world – since all
That Berlin can mobilise is thick wall –
That our army be a new horizon dawning!

EDMOND ROSTAND

# Driver Gunner

Now here I am free and proud among comrades
Reveille sounds it's dawn I wave a greeting
To that famed new day I've still never seen

```
      LET
   GO YOUR
  C*      C K S
 PUT      ON    BUNCH OF W*NKERS IT'S A NEW
 YO    UR  YOU    day              try
   FROCKS  YOU    sh*              un
              gg            co
               ing for your
```

The three servers arm in arm have nodded off on the limber
As driver on the near horse up hill down dale
Amble trot or gallop I steer the gun
The officer's arm is my pole star
It's raining my coat's soaked through from time to time I wipe
    my face
With the towel from the saddle-bag on the next horse
Here come infantry heavy tread muddy feet
They're stung by the needles of rain they're followed by their
    packs

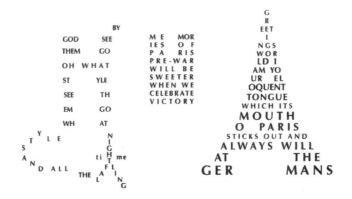

```
                              BY                        G
                                                        R
             GOD        SEE                            EET
                                                        I
             THEM       GO                             NGS
                                                       WOR
             OH  WHAT                                  LD I
                                      ME   MOR         AM YO
             ST         YLE           IES   O F        UR  EL
                                      P  A  RIS        OQUENT
             SEE        TH            PRE-WAR          TONGUE
                                      WILL BE         WHICH ITS
             EM         GO            SWEETER         MOUTH
                                      WHEN WE         O  PARIS
             WH         AT            CELEBRATE      STICKS OUT AND
                                      VICTORY       ALWAYS WILL
           T  Y  L  E        N                        AT      THE
          S                  I                       GER     MANS
          A  N      ti  H  me
             D ALL  THE F L
                      A  I
                         N
                          G
```

Infantrymen
Clumps of earth marching
You are the power
Of the soil that made you
And the soil it is that's on the move
When you advance
An officer gallops by
Like a blue angel in the grey rain
A wounded man walks smoking a pipe
The hare bolts and here's a brook I'm fond of
And carters that young woman's waving to us
Victory's clipped firmly to our helmets
And calculates the angles for our guns
Our storms of firing are its shouts of joy
Its flowers the flourished marvel of our shell-bursts
Its pondering the glory of our trenches

I HEAR THE SONG
O
U                OF birds
R
LOVELY RAPTORS

GUILLAUME APOLLINAIRE

# Execution

*To Sergeant Bordeau, who performed many such executions*

Itching all night long, it's never ended.
Stem the evil of the scratch:
In a shirt-seam, where they hatch,
One of the blackguards is apprehended.

The time has come, let justice be enacted,
In all its rigour, with all speed:
Against such unrepentant greed
Humanity has suddenly reacted.

Louse, your bliss was brief as mayfly's breath –
The verdict's quick, no pity is expressed,
The perpetrator is condemned to death

And fingernail to fingernail is pressed.
– A bit like us, as the war goes on:
One sharp crack, you're gone.

ANDRÉ MARTEL
Bois de Malancourt, April 1915

# Concert

How amusing,
   Zing!
Bullets in screams –
Malice, missing! –
   Sing
Cannibal dreams.

Gong that pealed
   Squealed,
Strings that flinched
Screeched and wheeled,
   Keeled,
Girls' bottoms pinched.

Whip and crack,
   Whack –
An army shoots
And quavers clack
   Wrack
From giant flutes.

Should the gun –
   Fun
We dread will come –
In fierce combat
   Clat-
ter giant drum,

Our faithful rifles-
   'll z-
ip out a trill,

A merry tune
   Soon
A joyful quadrille.

Allegretto,
   Soh!
Machine-gun six-eight
In rapid reels
   Deals
The Boche his fate.

With burning eyes
   Lies
Hun in defeat,
Croaks his death,
   Breath
Losing the beat,

The startled bane
   Slain –
Pink Boche pests
Face in the mire,
   Choir
Counting the rests.

We, when the song,
   Long
Sweetly euphonic
And free of faults,
   Halts
On the subtonic,

Lest sudden lah –
   Aargh! –

Bring fresh predation,
Fast launch the
       Re-
capitulation.

ANDRÉ MARTEL
Barrage, Bois de Malancourt, April 1915

## The Rains

Petroleum sings in streams
Of flame and plumes of infamy,
To the writhing screams
Of the man in agony –
Bellona's eager warfare
Supplying Pluto on the cheap.
It's raining fire. Shepherdess fair,
Come butcher your sheep.

Steel chops and hacks,
Amid the infernal blast,
At a man choking, racked
As he gasps his last.
Into the forests blare
Brass and copper, digging deep.
It's raining iron. Shepherdess fair,
Come butcher your sheep.

From exploding limbs and jaws
Flesh charred black is rent.
God, the fireworks that soar
When the shell-holes vent!

See, dark blobs of bloody glair –
Drink, greedy seeds, drink the seep,
It's raining blood. Shepherdess fair,
Come butcher your sheep.

Far from the hideous slaughter
Flows a river of tears in spate,
Delicious, slaking water
For the Kaiser of hate.
Women, weep and rend your hair;
Hun, in joy carouse and leap,
It's raining tears. Shepherdess fair,
Come butcher your sheep.

ANDRÉ MARTEL
Dombasles-en-Argonne, March 1915

# Bruiser

When the signal to attack was heard,
Emile, a mighty Burgundian, dubbed 'Bruiser',
Was out of the trench in a single bound,
Launching the assault with his comrades.

Amid the raging clamour of the cannon,
The crash of shells, the song of the machine-guns,
Amid the steel and fire, the mud, the blood,
The trees collapsing to the quivering earth,
Amid the swarming insect-buzz of splinters,
The men, each face a terrible fixed grin,
Cut their way through the entanglements,
Leapt shell holes through the choking gun smoke,

Boots muddily trampling smouldering flesh,
And dived like madmen full into the furnace.
Now the fifteen men were down to three,
Hurdling fallen bodies by the hundred.
The first went sprawling, intestines hot steam;
The second fell shot clean through the head
In the hurricane blast; but Bruiser
Ran on, breasting the black wind of death,
Alone, through the blare of shot and shrapnel.
Charging up a Boche sap, suddenly
He stopped, panting with the fevered excitement
Of a mettlesome horse reined in hard,
His beard a streaming fountainhead of blood.
Then, with a roar to swell the roar of steel,
Demon-like, he plunged into that deep hell.

He had no rifle now, and no grenades,
But still was raging forward, deaf to the din,
When a Hun with a knife flung himself
Head-first at Bruiser at a bend in the sap.
Thus, in their modern trench, did two cavemen
Play out the ancient drama of the forests.
An isolated man stumbled on the scene
And stopped in his tracks, appalled at the sight:
Tiger and lion, walled in, ferocious,
Men slashing open one another's guts.
– O Kaiser, cursed Emperor, dare to pale and blench!
Give some token of distress! Behold, and tremble! –
And, throats quivering in rage and pain,
A tangle of bleeding, steaming muscle,
The two weltered and choked on death together,
Locked mouth to mouth in horrible embrace.

ANDRÉ MARTEL
Dombasles-en-Argonne, May 1915

# Nocturne

The guns have fallen silent, gagged with fog,
in the winter's night that cancels space,
and a calm, full of menace
as the screech of owls over castle walls,
hangs in the many-hearted silence.

Sentries, peering out,
tense every muscle, edgily
awaiting the unexpected.

A thwack like wet cloth
sounds from the valley –
sudden muffled rifle-shots
unsure of guessed-at shadows
and the rustling emptiness.

Tonight
is like the nights in Breton legend
when hell-hag washerwomen
kneel invisible at riverside stones,
beating shrouds in the thick water.

ALBERT-PAUL GRANIER
Observation post, Meuse, 1915

## 'I always thought...'

I always thought that, clasped in a lover's arms,
      Being weak was heaven-sent,
And that soft surrender to a strong embrace
      Embraced with equal strength.

But now I hate – how I hate – my weakness.
      I hate these feeble wrists
That used to stroke him, smooth and sinuous
      In their bangles and bracelets,

And this lissome, living body, on a chain
      At the doors of empty dwellings,
That curls up and sleeps when cries of human pain
      And anguish fill the heavens.

CÉCILE PÉRIN

# Wartime April

The north wind whistling round the doors,
Snow, filling the lanes and tracks with white.
Wartime April, April caught
And pinioned with the gale's lash,
April of the stricken light.

The women wear black veils,
The girls a grown-up dignity.
The talk is in murmurs. Night
Closes in... Silence... A splinter
Of hope gleams in the dark, like driftwood.

Here we sit, no one speaking now.
What do you say to a woman crying?
Here we sit, like prisoners.
Never stirring, each in her house,
We sit, and know the men are dying.

CÉCILE PÉRIN

# For as Long and as Often as You Wish, Sir!

That's ten attacks we've mounted here, 'with no significant gains'.
And again, the General says? For as long and as often as you wish, Sir!

First a cigarette. A slug of wine goes down a treat! Cheers mate!
Too many of us still on our feet in this proud regiment.

Cheers, old mate! What were you in civvy street, back in those strange
    times when we were alive?
A barber? My father's in a bank, I'm pretty sure he was Monsieur
    Legrand.

Butcher, farmer, priest, lawyer, pedlar, cheesemonger, leather-cutter,
There's all sorts in the trench, as them across the way are soon going
    to find out!

All of us brothers like naked infants, all alike as peas in a pod.
In civvy street, well yes, we were all different, but once in the squad
    we're just simply *men*!

No father now, nor mother, no age, just a rank and a number,
Just the mate who knows what he and I have got to do, without delay,
    but not too soon either.

All that's behind me now is the second section, all that's with me a
    job to be done,
All that's before me now is the deafening consignment of thunder I've
    got to deliver!

Delivering my body and blood, delivering my soul to God,
Delivering to the gentlemen opposite this thing in my hand with their
    address on!

(For as long as there is someone in my skin, for as long as we've belts
   we can tighten,
For as long as there's that bloke opposite staring into my face!)

If the bomb does its work, what is one more human soul that's
   exploded?
And the bayonet is like a steel tongue, thrust out, tugging me on,
   straighter and thirstier than my own!

There's all sorts in the trench, just watch for when the officer gives
   the signal,
And what comes out will be France, terrible as the Holy Spirit!

For as long as there are those men across the way trampling what's
   ours under the soles of their boots,
For as long as there's this injustice, for as long as there's this force
   against the greater force that is justice,

For as long as there's one refusing to accept, for as long as there's
   one to see and to heed justice calling,
For as long as there's a Frenchman to laugh out loud and believe in
   all that's eternal,

For as long as there's a future we can lay on the table, for as long
   as we've a life to give,
Our lives and those of our nearest and dearest, my wife and children
   with me with their lives to give,

For as long as all that can stop a living man is steel and fire,
For as long as there's living French meat to march through all your
   damned barbed wire,

For as long as there's a woman's child to march through all your
   science and your chemistry,
For as long as with us the honour of France shines brighter than
   the sun at its zenith,

For as long as there is this great country behind us, listening, praying,
    staunch in silence,
For as long as our eternal vocation is to march over you, paunch
    and all,

– For as long and as often as you wish, completely, utterly, to the last
    man! For as long as there's a man still standing, the living and the
    dead together!
For as long and as often as you wish, Sir! O France, for as long, and
    as often, as you wish!

PAUL CLAUDEL
June 1915

# The Precious Blood

When he has consumed the bread, the priest receives the substance
    of Jesus Christ
        In liquid kind,
The body and the blood concomitant, God made as one with
    the body by the Word,
        Here in the chalice that the priest drains,
The Word, in this golden chalice, speaking to the Ineffable of what
    He is,
        The blood that is eternally the Word uttered,
God inside His creature's mouth, inside this heart where it pleases
    Him to be,
        This mouthful of real wine swallowed!
This blood, which He received from Mary, which he had in common
    with her,
        The warmth from His own heart,
Now in our turn infuses us, in the illuminating, intoxicating,
        Warm sun of sacrament.
O draught more penetrating than the mind, swifter all through us
    than fire,
        O cup of pure understanding,
Release at last the wellspring of penitence from this flesh I have
    so little use for,
        From this sealed heart.
The great eruption of thirst, the sickness, the lacerating, unassuaged
    desire
        Of one who loves You,
The cry, the plea, the indignation of one who prefers Another
    to himself,
        Beyond death, beyond life.
Blessed is he who, in the desert of the Cross and the sleep of Paradise,
        Shares in the Lord's death,
And tastes and makes his own at last the absolute of suffering,
        Through God's part therein.

What we raise in our two hands is not the golden chalice, but more:
   it is the whole
         Of Calvary, the Lord sacrificed.
What the Lord has put into our hands is not remembrance
   of His death, but more:
         It is His whole person.
Redemption whole, entire, as from a tilting vase,
         The Five Rivers of Paradise,
Divine preference in a flood all upon us, the other Life,
         To our lips, Life!
O Lord, for a glass of water, You promised us the boundless sea:
         Who knows if You also do not thirst?
And we know our blood, which is all we really have, is good to
   quench Your thirst,
         For You have told us so.
If there truly is a wellspring in us – well, we shall soon be finding out!
         For if there is virtue in this wine,
And if our blood is red, as You say it is, how can we see,
         Other than in our blood shed?
If our blood truly is as precious as You say, if it truly is as gold,
         If it is of use, why keep it?
Why forget all that can be bought with it, and hoard it like treasure,
         O my God, when You ask it of us?
We know our sins are great, and that absolutely we must do penance,
         But it is hard when a man weeps.
 Here, then, in place of tears, is our blood, which we have shed
   for France:
         Do with it as You please.
Take it, we give it to You, put it to Your own good use and profit,
         We ask nothing of You.
– But if You have as great a need of our love as we have need
   of Your Justice,
         Then, truly, Your thirst is great!

                                        PAUL CLAUDEL

# Possession

Sprawling, legs akimbo, flat on its face,
A grey-green heap of smear on the green grass,
This human relic crawling with horror,
Inert, this lump of flesh draped in squalor,
We know by just the one name – Boche. No matter:
A foe laid low is but a scrap of dead meat
That time and rain will slowly gnaw like leather
And the earth drag down into its larder.
O stranger, lowly soldier, nameless speck,
Faceless war-slave, in death more nameless yet,
Your race once bared its fangs in covetous lust
For this soil your teeth are thrusting at.
So, Conqueror by choice or by decree, do eat:
You have all eternity to chew your treat.

HENRY-JACQUES
'The Labyrinth', Artois, 1915

# The Horseman's Farewell

God yes! war's a lovely thing
With all the songs the lazy days
How I've rubbed and buffed this ring
I hear you sighing in the breeze

God bless! there's the call to go
He mounted turned off past the gate
Arrived and died while she at home
Sat smiling at the quirks of fate.

GUILLAUME APOLLINAIRE


# Earth Ocean

I've built a house out in mid-Ocean
Its windows are the rivers running from my eyes
Octopuses swarm all over where the walls are
Listen to their triple hearts beating and their beaks against the  windows
       House awash
       House aflame
       Time a-winging
       Time a-singing
     The planes are laying eggs
      Watch out they're dropping anchor
Watch out the dropping angry ink
Were you but from heaven
Heaven's honeysuckle climbs skyward
Earth's octopuses palpitate
And then there are so very many of us digging our own graves

Pale octopuses of the chalky waves pale-beaked octopuses
Around the house this ocean that you know my friend
And is never still

GUILLAUME APOLLINAIRE

## What's Where

There's a ship that's sailed away with my beloved
There are six sausages in the sky and with night coming they look like
    maggots hatching from the stars
There's an enemy submarine that bore my love ill will
There are a thousand little fir trees broken up by shell splinters all
    round me
There's an infantryman going by blinded by poison gases
There's the fact that we've completely smashed the Nietzsche Goethe
    and Cologne trenches
There's the fact that a letter I'm longing for still hasn't come
There are several photos of my love in my map case
There are the prisoners going by looking worried
There's a battery with the servers bustling round the guns
There's the mail orderly trotting up along Lone Tree Lane
There's a spy so it's said on the prowl round here as invisible as the
    horizon because he's contemptibly disguised in its blue and
    blended in with it
There's my love standing tall like a lily her bust a flower head
There's a captain anxiously waiting for wireless messages from mid-
    Atlantic
There are soldiers at midnight sawing planks for coffins
There are women screaming for maize by a bleeding Christ in Mexico
    City
There's the Gulf Stream so warm and benign
There's a cemetery full of crosses 5 kilometres from here

72

There are crosses scattered everywhere

There are prickly pears on those cacti in Algeria

There are my love's long supple hands

There's an inkwell I made from a 15-centimetre shell they wouldn't let
me post

There's my saddle exposed to the rain

There are the rivers not flowing back upstream

There's love gently carrying me along

There was a Boche prisoner carrying his machine gun on his back

There are men in the world who've never been in a war

There are Indians looking in astonishment at the landscapes of the
west

They are melancholically remembering people they wonder if they'll
ever see again

For in the course of this war great advances have been made in the art
of invisibility

GUILLAUME APOLLINAIRE

# Festival

Fireworks wrought with steel
That lighting's charm itself
    What pyrotechnique
Tinge bravery with gracefulness

High above
Two shells burst pink
Like the brazen thrust of nipples
From two breasts unbuttoned
HE DID LOVE
    Some epitaph

In the forest a poet
Indifferently watching
    Revolver holstered
Roses die from hoping

Thinks of Saadi's roses
Suddenly his head droops
For he's reminded by a rose
Of a curve of thigh soft smooth

The air's full of a ghastly alcohol
Filtering from the half-closed stars
The shells caress the soft
Nocturnal scent of your repose
    Gangrenous roses

GUILLAUME APOLLINAIRE

# All Souls' Day

Public mourning, unconsoled,
A landscape hunching drab and bare
Among the plundering flames of autumn,
Bells tolling, guns' thunder rolling,

All Souls' Day, day of graveside prayer,
Bells tolling, guns' thunder rolling,
Our wearying hearts grown dull and numb
To bells, the alarms, and everywhere

Entire tragedies of lives undone.
In the sad, soft wind, we feel
Brush round us as we kneel
Dead leaves and sundered souls.

At last the bells pause for breath;
But not the drumming, willing guns –
While we are celebrating death,
The distance dins with killing, killing.

LUCIE DELARUE-MARDRUS

# Poor Dogs

Round the pitiful villages,
round the burnt-out hamlets,
the dogs, the poor bewildered dogs, go mutely padding
to and fro among the shell-holes,
searching for the doorstep,
searching through the scattered rubble
and collapsed roofs,
stepping over charred beams,
sniffing uncertain scents.

The poor dogs' friendly eyes,
innocent and gentle,
implore the soldiers:
'Tell me, please tell me,
where's the rough and ready master,
the kindly mistress,
the little children who played with me?'
– those friendly amber eyes questioning,
innocent and gentle…

The poor lost dogs pad soundlessly like shadows
to and fro in villages of rubble,
like memories in madmen's heads.

ALBERT-PAUL GRANIER
1915

## Military Bands

Military bands,
The roll of drums,
Fanfares of bugles, fanfares full-winged
And filling with the morning winds –
How they pound, the hearts of men!

Military bands,
Along the roads at dawn,
Lit by the clear blue sky filling with light:
Over the fields and meadows and misty woods,
With wispy fog rising from the river
How crystal-bright you sound
In the light from the clear blue sky!
Military bands,
You march through the streets, intoxicate the streets,
The cobbles hot from the soldiers' boots,
And with you go the wayside passers-by,
Whisked away,
With the watchers from the windows
Snatched up and swept along,
Eyes shining,
Lives filling with a wind of heroism.

And the soldiers? Yes, the soldiers
March, on they march, heads held high,
Courage in their eyes, a glow in their hearts,
Wrapped round in fanfare,
And straighten their backs under the packs,
A new spring in their weary step,
Marching to the station, the trains, and
Off and away...

In their uniforms
– Their uniforms,
Faded, filthy, rumpled, frayed, torn,
But it still is the uniform,
And these exhausted men who wear it
Have closed together,
Skin to skin, elbow to elbow,
One brute spirit irresistibly
Still uniting and lifting these weary men –

In their uniforms, out
Under the heady billowing flags,
In the fiery whirlwind song
Of bugles sounding the attack,
In the thunderous pounding of the drums,
Oh! in all the din, the fire, the dying,
The bullets, the shells, the shrapnel,
The flashing, slicing steel,
On they press, leaving you mad bands behind,
Forgetful of self and all else,
On into the flaring darkness –
And death, stock-still, ice-cold, unveils
Its hellish silence.

Death!
Death! Whole battalions have cracked and broken,
And already, from under each man's corpse,
Each and every solitary dead man,
Each gaunt corpse in tattered uniform,
– Oh, you're silent now, military fanfares –
There rises the human soul,
Rises horror-stricken, naked,
Set free, alone,
Into the night, the silence, the frozen fixity,
A soul regretful, the soul of memory...

Military bands,
Where now the hot and heady roll of drums?
The dead, these corpses, the dead –
*You* brought them to this,
And now, and now
The man from before your time,
With his everyday life,
The trade that earned him his bread,
The mother who bore him,
His sorrows, joys and loves,
That life of humble grandeur,
A life of warmth, a life of beauty,
With his everyday life,
That is the man who is dead.

Oh, you're silent now, military fanfares,
Breath blown, an ice-cold wind over graveyards;
Now let the death of that man be accounted,
The value of his life, against his death.

Dying…
To die! To have known how to live and loved life,
To scorn death and run to meet death
And die with no regrets and die with joy,
Knowing how good life was and how enchanting,
And that all shall founder and death take all
– I hail you, soldiers, victors or vanquished,
Whose worthy lives demanded such a death
As their crowning glory,
I hail all you who, knowing you would die,
And regretting nothing, reviling nothing
From so loved a life, yet sought out death.

O you who died on the barricades,
Whose blood spattered the cobbled streets of cities,

You willing dead, I hail you. Of you I say:
Happy are these dead.
They died elated, yes, but lucid,
Embracing death with a giddy elation
They had distilled from all their love for life,
Resolutely choosing death, their free,
Their final choice, their death indeed a *dying*.

Happy they who died to crown their lives with glory.
– Military bands, alien intoxication,
Happy they who died in joy and never heard you,
Their radiance having no need of your light,
They whose dying day was a day in their lives
Like all their other days and the worthiest of all,
Happy they who died looking death in the eye,
Their soul and conscience clear, and with all their soul,

Happy they who died in workers' clothes.

MARCEL MARTINET

# The Attack

*To Captain Grillet*

'You there, behind the parapet,
what are you men doing?'

     'Sir, spring's coming, Sir:
birds darting among the branches,
only, this year
they're so quick you can't see them —
and these birds buzz, like bees!'

     'Sir, take cover, Sir,
why don't you take cover?'

     'What a racket!
               Ah, the bastards –
bullet through my water bottle, and it was full!'
        'And that gas of theirs is parching!'
        'Too bad, I'll eat snow –
what's left between the shell-holes
and isn't poisoned…'

Steel is mattocking the white earth,
turning it over in blasts of smoke;
the earth erupts like rockets through the branches
and falls back, black, on the snow,
gesticulating roots.

Evening thunderstorms in cities,
fat raindrops on glass canopies,
loud, splatting raindrops,
gale-force nights at sea,
high waves against the cliffs:

this evening, these are all become steel hatred –
this ferocious, nightmare evening.

The steel squeals in the seething air,
chiselling fluted columns of noise
with shell-bursts for capitals:
The steel's fierce mattocking goes on
in a frenzy of splinters
that hackles up the flesh of the trees.

The air is gritty with explosions,
then smoothed by the cool flight of the Austrian shells,
like a musical caress,
a caress of oboes and fifes,
with the pizzicato bass continuo
of heavy mortars in the distance,
as the seventy-fives blare
and the one-twenty timps give the orchestra a beat.

      'Whop! Wham! – Sir,
we're not in time;
Whop! Wham! the dance is whipping up:
whoever is it dances to this –
Death?'
      'Whop! Wham! Timpanist, you're insane –
don't thump your skins so hard,
timpanist, you're nowhere near in tune!
Come on, tune up, give those keys a twist!
Here, the thunder'll give you an A!'

      'Whop! Wham! The timpanist's insane!'

      'What? Still no contact?
None of the runners back,
and no one any idea
what that machine-gun's jabbering?'

'Right. Time for goodbyes, Sir.'
'Coming with me, lad?
Good man, thanks.

Well, let's go!'


'Whop! Wham! What a lovely symphony –
is it Dukas, d'Indy, d'Udadidynkiki??'
'But the orchestra really are insane –
not one of them's keeping time
and the timpani's not in tune!'

Whop! Wham! The orchestra's insane!
And wielding the baton is Death.

ALBERT-PAUL GRANIER
Verdun (Bois des Fosses, Bois d'Hardaumont),
21–24 February 1916




# From *The Poem of the Trench*

'The Day' (closing section)


[…]


In the forward trench, one foot on the fire-step,
Like dead men waking in their graves, they slowly
Rise, and see, with every shell that falls,
Wood and sandbags flying.

Sinister trains climb hissing through the sky,
Then clatter back down into distant buffers.
Parapets collapse in sulphurous clouds,
But no one hears the cries.

Grenades at the ready or bayonets fixed,
They're waiting, pale-eyed, practically deafened;
In their helmets they all look the same,
      Blank, immune to pity.

All that's in them now is one fierce desire.
No wife would ever now know the man
Whose mouth so often groaned love into hers.
      They clamber up and out.

          *

      Now see our age-old soil
      All at once erupt –
          Its noblest magma,
      Its young, most living hope!
      See the sap boil up
From the tree that fate chopped back,
      The naked steel shine out
Like a new branch, strong and straight.
See the swarm, out from the hive.
See our day's light pressing forward,
Armed with the counsels of the night.
      The wolf has broken cover –
See hounds and huntsmen spring to chase.
      The dough is fully worked –
Here's the heat to bake the bread.
      The woodman's felled the tree –
Here, to finish off the job,
Come the craftsmen carpenters.

          *

      Reason slackens grip,
      Fogs over, abdicates;

What they improvise today
They'll have forgotten by tomorrow.
On they run, heads down, delivered
To the whim of some dark Spirit...
And yet, O Lord, this blind tragedy
　　Was written in thy Book.

*

　　　　Mine explodes,
　　　　Spits black fire.
　　　　Wild eyes wide,
　　　　Firing blind.

　　　　The soil drinks deep.
　　　　Rat-tat – the mincer!
　　　　A wife's a widow,
　　　　A son's an orphan.

　　　　'Ammo, quick!'
　　　　Mouths' shouts
　　　　Lost in din.
　　　　Sudden night
　　　　Shuts thirty eyes.

　　　　Like a school kid
　　　　Chucking stones,
　　　　The bomber clears
　　　　A bloody path.

　　　　Heaven shield you,
　　　　Blameless hand!

*

Cutter cuts,
Rifle fires,
Platoon at work
On its own.

Quick hiss
Through grass,
Corporal trips,
Corpse drops.

Foot snags,
Nearly there.

Ladder pitched
By one man,
Another man's
Already up,
Here come the rest.

In every sap
Gun butts thump,
Knives glint.

\*

Earth walls to left and right,
Man in grey and man in blue
In this tight valley
Meet before God.

Evening now. A landscape
All of four feet square.

Remember this face,
Its horror-struck eyes.

Remembering, say nothing
Of this waxen fake.

The face a blackening mask already.

Remember, resolving not to speak,
And so to emulate the earth,
Which tells no stories.

*

The grass is asking to be cleansed.
Go, man in blue, search and probe,
But let pity stay your hand
If the man in grey should kneel.

Though every ditch is full of dead,
Keep on, trampling, stepping over.
The stream has stained its banks with red,
Night's falling and the sky's in flames.

Flares dazzle, white and green,
And your strength's completely drained –
How does the world look to you now,
By the light of signal rockets?

In their pale, brief, falling flash,
How does your house look to you now?
And your friends? The dreams you had?
Do you recognise yourself?

What's left, tonight, of the spirit
And the heart that once you had?
A body drags along,
A weeping voice fades...

Hands scrabble earth, a spurt of oily flame
    Floods out, tans shredded hides.
We cry to thee, O Lord: this agony
    Makes sweet the darkness of the grave.


    Each second sees the horror
Grow as grows the flame, and the groans of pain.
The men, exhausted, are shut off from the world
    By curtains of explosion.


The great dark wave for a moment is repulsed,
Then foams back up the shore to the cliff's foot.
The Night in sudden rage has reared again
    And snuffed the Day's work out.


Three times, in deadly, frontal mass attacks,
    Comes the surge of men,
Some vanishing into black opacity,
    Some briefly flash-lit.
Three times, the men in grey scramble to the top,
    In vain:
Three times, their column gives, slithers back down
    The steep ravine.


    A beam of light sweeps
      Field and hedge.
      In the tensed
      Rise and dip,
    Eyes stare, faces whiten.


The calls of the dying go unheard.


The hand reloads the weapon, the head tilts,
The crater's a grinder, the handle's cranked,

The escarpment's red,
Then black… then red… black.

Everywhere, from churned-up graves
Come earth-caked
Bloody corpses from the early days.
Feverishly, an arm
Plugs a breach.
Such thirst! Throats parched!

All time has ceased; courage, fear –
A single, addled numbness.
Rifle's burning hot.
Firing's never stopped…

Until, up in front, like an ebbing flood
Leaving puddles in the fields,
The last of the men in grey have vanished,
Slump-shouldered, back into the woods
And, over the dead men, the ripped-out timbers,
The collapsing doorways, the splintered trees,
Bit by bit, the screaming air falls silent.


'The Day After'

The night is thick with rain
Trampling softly everywhere.

One shivers,
Another sobs,
The third does nothing, says nothing.

'Who are you, then?'

89

The scattered flock are counted.
How many are there
On the brink of darkness,
Eyes flickering shut?

How many are there, suffering
On this hill?

How many, uncomprehending
Souls, simple and accepting?

They are alive:
They would be famished
Had they not
This need to sleep, and sleep, for ever.

Their only kiss the endless
Wind against their faces,
And still the rain, and still the mud,
The never-ending.

All but drained of strength,
And never any respite;
All that's left, in that poor, emptied skin,
The dreaming spirit.

Just a glimmer somewhere in the heart,
After all the frenzy,
Just enough to register
The whole thing is about to start again.

Just enough blood in an empty vein
To watch, and wait for dawn,
And finally, tomorrow, gift this last,
Still pulsing, trickle.

\*

First light, a dirty, soggy yellow,
Like soupy puddles on a beach,
Finds them changed past recognition,
Fifteen of them, slumped in a hole.

Their uniforms are now the colour
Of the sandbags and the earthworks;
And yet they do still have their voices,
Muffled, dull, down in their throats.

With difficulty, their tongues shape
The odd slow word, thick and hoarse:
Occasionally, a dead man's name
Is passed among the streaming helmets.

Time passes; a cloud bursts overhead;
Fog forms, catches on the tree;
They sit, and wait for the relief,
    And share their bread.

\*


Let us stand, bare-headed, in respect,
    Before these men, and know our place,
    For we ourselves are unworthy;
    Let us, in them, love France herself,
    As it is fitting she be loved:
With solemnity and reverence.

Be it in the old cockaded tricorne,
    Or the guardsman's heavy bearskin,
    Or the infantryman's shako,

Or, today once more, the sallet,
   Or, shouldering the hod again,
Tomorrow, in the vintager's soft hat,

This France is a France but little known,
   Austere, profound and unadorned,
   Like the dark soil of fresh ploughland;
   Distrustful of grandiloquence,
   She prefers to odes and sonnets
An inner, heartfelt fervour never told.

It is never she who trumpets forth
   Those sacred words: Mother, and Country;
   With all the stubborn steadiness
   Of the farmer at his plough,
   She says nothing, and her courage
Is like a simple, unembellished wall.

FRANÇOIS PORCHÉ
January–May 1916

# The Young Man's Death

As he left, abloom with soaring hope,
For an uncertain desert place where life
Would have the warm and fertile faith of vines,
The youth with eyes of gold was felled by base iron,
Soul dashed down, chest gashed as by a knife,
Tangled in the wire, throat torn open.

    He'll never have that frown,
That endless rancour of one joylessly
Dozing under a green tree, uninspired
To wonder whether April's strawberry-stained –
For he must watch, that ever French remain
The forest of luminous, treacherous wire
Where the lovely huntress Death ruthlessly
    Let fly and brought him down.

And we who are left, by sweet pride driven,
Wandering, await that same brave death:
Our flesh a brandished axe, our final breath
Drawn in horror's spite, lives freely given.

GABRIEL-TRISTAN FRANCONI<br>February 1916

# The Flag of Revolt

O brothers unknown, I speak in your name,
Who dare not clamour forth your bitter suffering,
Who die, without a word, all hope long since snuffed out,
For peoples led – misled – by men of shame.

O weeping parents, I speak in your name,
Who mourn a son for whom death came as sweet release,
Who can no longer, in your unremitting grief,
Believe the mortal lies of those men of shame.

I speak in your name, friends silent in your graves,
Who feed this hecatomb in endless waves,
Who shall rise from the earth when Truth conquers falsehood.

In all your names, I call upon the masses
To raise at last, above a world collapsing,
The Flag of Revolt – the Flag of Brotherhood!

MARC DE LARREGUY DE CIVRIEUX
At the front, March 1916

## 'The lieutenant is asleep...'

The lieutenant is asleep in the metal cabin,
Despite the sun resounding off the sea
And the footsteps ringing between decks.

The galley floor is glistening with grease;
But while one man, standing in a doorway,
Buffs the bottom of a pan with fine sand,
Another kneels and, with a shard of glass,
Sniffing, scrapes the muck up off the steel.

And other men, perching on a trestle,
Sew the regulation buttons on.

Looking out to port, someone spots,
Between a winch and a ventilator shaft,
A dumpy ship that's making too much smoke.

How far away it is now, that peaceful Asian sea.
The eye has to rub up this glittering velvet water
And smooth right out each crease in the waves.

\*

A great denuded plateau, out of kilter,
Strangely humped and hollowed all across.
Contours now quite meaningless, obsolete.

Sloughed skin, a relic! No one's country now.
Even the horizon holds no promise.
The land is no guide, and the muddy sky
Vouchsafes no hint of where the sun might be.

Yet there's something, stretching away,
Somewhat worn and battered,
Not a track, just a trace;
A memory of long-gone footsteps.

The leading horse's nostrils
Knowingly sniff the hint;
And the tugging bridles
Jerk their stocky riders.

Every horse in one column
Has stumbled on the same rock,
While alongside trotted
An earth-complexioned figure.

Praise be! A Mongol horde
Is on its way to Europe's war.

*

Two trains have stopped, one behind the other,
Two black tubes, each packed with a thousand men.

A plain reaches out as far as the eye can see;
The ground looks soggy under the short grass,
Water tracing little channels all round.
Stagnant sun, mosquitoes swimming in it,
Leaves each swamped, low compartment heat-drunk:

Two battalions soaking in a sleep
That smells of painted wood and brought-up food.

*

But other fleets inventively
Are feeling out subtle new routes.

There is one in the tropics,
Its cladding warping in the heat;

Another pushing its ten bows
Through the pack-ice rubble.

Other columns are on the move
Across a more rugged desert.

Trains are whistling at other signals.

But all are marching to the same death.

JULES ROMAINS

## 'Anxiety…'

Anxiety, an anguish, high in the chest,
A sickening, slow churn;
                          anxiety
Like a prisoner locked in for life.

The inmost seat of joy powerfully gripped
And squeezed like a fruit someone's trying to burst.

A thought inside me trapped and dying somewhere
Of thirst and horror in the padlocked flesh.

A distress inside me too big for my body.

The heat, the end-of-day murk, the air
Against the cheek like a sweaty, dirty hand.
More an anti-climax than a twilight.
The street dark, beyond all consolation.

Men sitting in dim bars, drinking out
The time that's left to them, second by second.

The bottom of the glass looming horribly.

A dusty breath sweeping all life up
Into the spiral gulf of a corridor.

A sudden zigzag split right through the present.

The spirit sensing, with a start, imminent
Departure, separation, oblivion.

Men slumped on benches in a waiting room;
The packs and the rifles; and eyes still living.
A force, a fluid, pushing at all as one,
Deeper into the meshing wheels and cogs.

Cities pressing, pushing at all as one.

JULES ROMAINS

# Fresh Supplies

The road grows wider day by day, floods into
The fields, as if to push the trees aside;
And along the scar-faced road, through pits
Of muddy urine marinating rubble,
Past crumbling walls, past abandoned houses
Bitten at by fire's jaded tooth,
Splashing the embankments into slurry,
Roll endless lorries packed with human meat.

For these are men no longer, but a single
Shapeless, soft mass, faces with no soul,
Eyes that judder open with every jerk,
Mouths that suddenly chew or swig or sing,
Simply to beguile the foul weather.
Bread or wine, rain or shine – no matter,
As long as hearts still beating somewhere prove
That life threads yet through the frail, imperilled flesh!

Those hills, so bare, stifling all the sound from
Obscure murdering that gags its victims,
Those fields, so gorged with blood, ploughed by crime into
Muck the pointless brawling thrashes in,
Grimly, humbly, almost blushingly,
A carnage none would know of but for the roads
And the plain all round, like blotting-paper –
That's where they're bound for, prime, unknowing cattle!

Here's a man will die tonight, while this one
Won't, but the one next to him will be killed;
The rest will wait their turn, for destiny
And death, its special friend, have a cushy job.
The massacre's all planned, worked out well ahead:

A hundred yards of earth, and glory-talk.
They've gone. More coming. All's absorbed into
The starless night, with its tormented lightning.

Death has soaked them through already, like oil
Rising through the wick ready for the flame.
And when they feel the ground beneath their boots,
Away from the jolts, the jumbled bodies,
Woken by the weight of pack and weapon,
They'll separate, each man aware he goes
Tonight to face an executioner who's
In a rage, fuming at the wealth of choice.

With no flags or bugles, War's gone to ground
To chew away the very world's living flesh,
Its appetite and health both in the pink.
O War, from your armies, endlessly renewed
Like tribes of rats breeding in ships' bowels,
Gorge and swill, unheeding of tomorrow –
For you have rations here for months to come!

The universe observes us; washes its hands.

GEORGES CHENNEVIÈRE
Verdun, March 1916

# The Passion of Our Brother the Poilu

'E were just a orn'ry Poilu
Servin' in the infantry.
Didn' want nowt to do wi' it –
'No ta, they've got it in fer me!'
But – yer gotta go, yer gotta go;
So up 'e got an' off 'e went,
'Cos 'e knew there ain't no point
In tryin' ter 'ave a argument,
'Cos the lads as till the soil
Is them as should defend it,
Even knackered territorials…
It's obvious, when's all's said an' done –
Can't all be makin' ammunition:
It's only workers, else them lawyers,
Can do their duty on the 'ome front!
Riskier out 'ere, I tell yer:
At the real front, in the trenches,
Any shells as yer can see,
Fact is they're most likely en'my –
It's only our artillery
See ours (better'n Boche 'uns though).

The Poilu set off wi' 'is mates
Wi' grenades fer the forward posts.
Foul night fer that kind o' caper,
Snowin', slippy an' pitch dark:
An' ev'ry step, wi' all the shell-'oles,
You was over on yer arse,
An' these was craters – real 'ell-'oles!
An' they was ev'rywhere, all round,
Like there were more 'ole than ground.

Suddenly there's a two 'undred ten
Bursts not twenty yard away.
'God, I'm 'it,' 'e yells, 'n' then
Goes down, 'n' crumples on 'is knees,
An' tips right over, an' 'e sees
'Is side ripped open an' 'is blood
Pumpin' out in a great spray...
'E says ter the corporal: 'It'd be good
If yer could tell the wife fer uz:
Jus' tell 'er... fer now... as I'm sick...
So's it's not jus' sprung on 'er, like.
There's a few francs in me pack...
Gi' 'em... gi' 'em the lads... An' don' forget
Me sack o' bombs... don' leave 'em behind...'
That's 'is last will 'n' testament –
An' then 'e passed away, peaceful like.

So there's 'is soul flyin' through the night –
No compass, but 'igh up in the sky
'E soon comes ter Paradise.
On the doorstep there's Saint Peter,
Whackin' carpets wi' a beater,
An' first thing is 'e roars at 'im:
'Wipe yer feet when yer get inside,
An' g'down the corridor on yer right.
'All o' Judgement's at the far end –
Sit on the bench an' they'll send fer yer!'
The poor Poilu's tremblin' all over;
When 'e gets there, there's a Angel in white
Asks 'im 'is name an' number
'N' 'is rank 'n' length o' service 'n' all –
This ain't what 'e'd been expectin'!
Poor lad's stood there in the 'allway
When the Angel says: 'They're ready fer yer.'

There 'e were in a kind o' church,
But 'e'd never seen owt like it,
It were red an' gold all over…
Then 'e spots, up the far end,
God Isself, sat on a star,
Wi' Jesus an' the 'Oly Virgin,
An' bushels o' candles all round,
An' loads o' Saints a bit lower down…
Most o' 'em was milit'ry men,
Wi' 'elmets an' armour an' spears –
Saint George, Saint Hubert an' Saint Leonard,
Saint Charlemagne wi' 'is beard,
Saint Maurice wi' 'is companions,
An' Joan o' Arc wi' 'er banner –
'N' Saint Michael, sat on 'is devil
(Who did not look 'appy), an' Saint Marcel…
When 'e sees all them soldiers
'E says t'isself: 'It's a court martial,
It's the works, I'm gonna cop it!'
But 'e couldn't no 'ow 'op it –
An' what a cross-examination:

'Right, now, tell me 'bout yerself,'
Says God ter the poor lad,
'What did yer do before the war?'
'Well, God, Sir, I ploughed the land;
Yer don' make money, that's fer sure,
'N' I weren't what yer might call well off,
But if yer work yer make enough,
An' I didn' never starve:
'Ad a pair o' bullocks, 'n' a 'orse,
'N' a cow, 'n' a wife, 'n' a few 'ens,
An' a pig – no offence – '
'Ah,' says Saint Anthony, 'Ah yes,
I know all 'bout pigs, o' course –

Brother, I give yer me blessin'!'
But God ain't 'appy, an' 'E frowns,
An' Saint Anthony, 'e pipes down…
'An' since yer started in the army,
I trust yer ain't done too much wrong?'
'A bit, God, but the list ain't long:
I sometimes did 'ave the odd skinful –
But where I'm from it ain't that sinful,
'N' honest, the wine were watery stuff –
Could 'ave too much, it still weren't enough.'
('Ere old Noah, the patriarch,
Sings out: 'Tha' ain't no great sin at all –
If I'd 'ave 'ad ter make the call,
I'd just 'ave said: "Yeah, float the Ark!"')
'Then once, they put me in the jail.
Bu' I reck'n I were in the right.
I'd split me breeches, as was too tight,
So, ter stop me bum comin' through,
I cut bits out me greatcoat tails,
An' sewn 'em on as good as new –
'N' the cap'n put me in the cooler
On account of I were guilty
O' damage ter Gov'ment property!'
Saint Martin says: 'Well, I tell yer,
That's just what I done meself,
The time I cut up me own tunic
To clothe a 'elpless paralytic –
'N' I got can'nised fer it, too!'
'They chucked the book at *me*,' says Poilu,
''Cos I'd gone an' made me *own* clothes;
Diff'rent system, I suppose…
Another time, I'd that many lice
I couldn' kill 'em all, 'n' the rest all grumbled –'
'Nah, yer shouldn' try an' kill 'em,'
Says Saint Labre, 'Do what I done,

104

Love 'em, 'n' scratch – 'elps keep yer 'umble.'
(But Saint Michael reck'ns that's vile,
An' sends 'im packin' down an aisle.)

'So yes, Lord, I 'ave done bad things,
Bu' I've 'ad stuff 'appen ter me, sad things,
'Ad ter put up wi' a pile o' stuff,
'Ad me share o' sufferin' –
Cold an' 'unger – *an'* the 'eat,
'Ad nights I never got no sleep;
Many's the time on them 'ard roads
I've took all the skin off me feet
Jus' marchin' – never-endin' marchin',
'N' sweatin' like a pig – beg pardon –
Wi' carryin' them 'eavy loads!
Sometimes, when it were real steep,
I've took mates' packs on top o' mine,
Just ter 'elp 'em out – yer know…
– Not as though I weren't knackered, mind!'
An' Saint Simon softly mutters:
'Jus' like us, Lord, at Golgotha…'
'So 'ere I am, up before Yer,
A naked soul, a 'omeless soul;
Lord, Lord, if I 'ave sinned,
Ain't I more 'n made amends?
– Lost all me blood… pale as death…
– An' look at the 'ole in me side!'
An' Saint Thomas says: 'In truth,
Our Lord Jesus 'ad the like!'

An' bein' as how God said nowt,
The Poilu raised 'is 'and an' shown 'Im
The Virgin's dress, as were blue,
An' God's own white beard, too,
An' Jesus's robe, as were red:

'Them there's my three colours!' 'e said,
'Them there's the colours o' France,
An' it were all fer France I suffered;
Them there's the colours o' me Flag,
The three colours o' me Country
As I got meself bled white fer –
France, my Country as I died fer,
'N' it's fer 'er I'm 'ere before Yer,
On me knees, Eternal Father!'

'N' then the Lord God smiled, an' motioned
As the gates of 'Eaven opened...

'N' the Poilu seen the 'Eavenly 'Ost
'Ad loads an' loads o' new recruits:
Sittin' revellin' in the leisure
Was poilus, sportin' sky-blue suits
As you'd o' thought was made ter measure,
An' 'elmets made o' solid gold;
Every one had wings ter fly,
So's never again t'ave boots full o' mud,
'N' even after a 'undred mile
Never again 'ave feet turned ter blood...

'N' the Poilu took 'is place among 'em,
'N' joined in wi' 'em as they sung:
'Glory ter God in the 'ighest!'
An' the Angels, in the light,
Answered 'em from every side:
'An' on Earth let there be Peace
Where men o' goodwill reside.'

MARC LECLERC
March 1916, Verdun

# Marching

So grey. So cold.
A monotony of rain
Stitching sky to roofs.
I think of a sleeping child's bare feet.

So grey. So cold.
Rats nibbling my bread,
Dawn shivering with me.
I send a kiss to two sleeping eyes.

So cold. So grey.
Go back to sleep in the fog
Over you like a sheet.
The cold rifle shocks my hand awake.

So cold. All grey,
Willows, partridge, plain.
March on, useless man!
I think of two unstirring arms.

So grey. Daybreak.
Dawn bleaching the stones.
My body marching blindly.
I send a kiss to two opening eyes.

So grey. So cold,
This day profaned already
By those mindless trumpets!
I think of tomorrow: just the same…

GEORGES CHENNEVIÈRE
1916

# The Flame

In this subterranean dark,
Lit by the devotional flame
Of just one short candle stub,
I draw warmth from your love.

I like this dingy, stony corner,
My love, for here I'm close to you,
And I can fill it with the secret
Of all my heart and soul.

Not the smell of sweat, nor the dust,
Nor the vermin, nor the mud
Shall ever soil this sanctuary
Where the true fire burns.

A jutting jaw beneath a helmet,
A back, hunching under the drab,
Two disembodied, idle hands
Is all they see of me.

My companions here, my brothers,
Why call on me to justify
My place among you and my silence?
A like treasure is in you.

Alas, the one I carry with me,
The one I clasp against my heart
And display for you to see,
Glows for my eyes only.

The most powerful force on earth
Has gathered, to my summons, within
This inward kingdom which follows me
Everywhere I go

And over which, as whistling death
Scours the craters of the plain,
With all my strength of heart and soul
I keep a still, silent vigil.

GEORGES CHENNEVIÈRE
Curlu, July 1916

# The Ladies Speak

They say: well yes, of course,
It's sad. All those young men!
And they haven't always the care they need. One simply can't, after all.
Our friend who did hospital work
(The one with the Military Cross)
Told us about it. Oh, it is sad.

But, good gracious, really,
If one listened to that Barbusse fellow
– That Latzko, says the one sitting opposite –
Oh, no, no, dear. That would be *too* dreadful.

Because after all, if it really were as they say it is,
So very awful,
We simply couldn't bear it,
We're not so hard-hearted.
It simply isn't possible.

In any case, my brother-in-law – he's a Captain –
Said in a letter that people do overstate it…
And then, there are wonderful moments,
When they're fired with enthusiasm – you know, when they attack?
Another cup of tea, dear?
(We still have a little sugar laid by.)

MARCEL MARTINET

# The Womenfolk

Left at home are the baby-machines,
The breeders bred to perpetuate the race.
Their happiness dies when their lovers leave;
They meekly stay behind and know their place.

Their battle is to clean the house, and weed;
The cupboard and the cellar are their troops;
Their victories: the washing and the soup;
Their mission: keep things tidy, knit, and breed.

Oh thankless, oh ironic, catch:
It's to protect their home and their hearth,
It's for them and their latest brat
That their sons and husbands charge to their death!

For them? So why, when the decisions are made,
Are their needs and wishes never weighed?
They're lucky they're allowed to suffer and fear:
Their share is waiting, and silence, and tears.

Women, does despair tear at your heart?
Dead, your son; dead, your husband. Just don't start –
Niobe's tears are permitted no more,
So hold your tongue, go back in and shut the door.

Time was when red-blooded ladies
Had the heart and stomach of a knight;
And they it was who judged the fight
And bestowed the victor's wreaths they'd made.

Today, you're held on tight legal rein,
Passionate creatures in forced passivity,
Each in her stall, a spirit bowed with pain,
Speech muzzled, strength tethered in inactivity.

[4 lines censored]

So here you stay, idle-handed, dutiful,
Noble Penelopes elegantly prinking –
Yes, you *are* still allowed to be beautiful,
And to read the papers, so you know what you're thinking,

And to show yourselves round hospital beds,
Or even be nurses in dressing stations –
You have to have contacts, of course, and not be low-bred,
Know the odd bishop, and make a donation.

So here you are, manacled in pretty fripperies
That none of you can even feel. Flatteries
Flutter down around you from the skies –
You're bound, you're gagged, with treachery and lies!

[29 lines censored]

HENRIETTE SAURET

# Riverside Walk

This path is strewn with dead leaves
Blown all over by dismal October;
Dreary autumn smacks and slaps
Its wings at the bare poplars' limbs,

And under its louring, birdless sky
The cold stones are rasped by crunched
Dead leaves, or muffled in the soft
Smell of rot from dead leaves.

You who walk this gloomy path,
Mothers, daughters, lovers, sisters:
Breathe deep the smell of rot,
Hear well the leaves' complaint –

There are places where October's winds
Are howling rain through bare forests,
And along the roads, down the banks,
Under bare bushes, are dead leaves,

And all that way away – in those forests
Your own poor feet will never take you to,
All along the never-ending roads
You will never know the names of,

Under the dead, dried-out, rotting leaves
October's winds are piling in the ditches –
Rotting in their beds of reddened leaves
Are the cold corpses of the men you love.

MARCEL MARTINET

## 'And you sleep in peace...'

And you sleep in peace; and do not feel
Press on your brows the world's desolation.
And you eat in peace; and do not hear
Sound through the dark the world's lamentations
As they rise and die. And you do not see
The million graves, black pits of devastation.

But I watch you, and listen to you drone
About your dreary pleasures. The wool no longer
Flicks through the fingers that 'did their bit at home'
All that first winter. And the great word War
Is just one among the homespun monotone
(You do, from time to time, touch on the war).

CÉCILE PÉRIN

## Market

Comings, goings, bustlings to and fro
    With a 'How are you, Madame?'
And 'Lovely morning!' 'Aren't things dear though!'
    'But one has to eat, Madame!'

There is a mass of peonies on the stalls,
    Piles of pink and red; peonies;
And slender women swaying home under stacks
    Of flowers. There are peonies.

And the war, of course. But so far away.
    A lovely day, you just forget.
A long way off, and no real news for days…
    – How might they all *not* forget?

CÉCILE PÉRIN

# The Ladies' Peace

Margaret of Austria and Louise of Savoy,
Seeing Kingdom and Empire sapped by endless war,
Journeyed, unescorted, unadorned, to Cambrai,
There to resolve the conflict, woman to woman.

Neither seeing in the other an enemy,
Above all partisanship and barren hatred,
Their first concern the sufferings of so many,
These two women were united.

For sure, they will have wept together
Over all the pointless deaths;
They will have cursed the stubbornness
Of minds degenerate with rancour.

Sincerely, with no caprice or cant,
In calm discussion of the issues,
They formulated the conditions
Of the delightful Ladies' Peace.

I love the grace and thoughtfulness of this accord.
Who, today, might have the intelligence and wit
To emulate that depth of common sense and wisdom
On which you drew, Princesses, centuries ago?

HENRIETTE SAURET
1916

# 'Since the Marne...'

Since the Marne, and then the fright
We got at Charleroi, I've dragged my bones
For endless miles along these roads;
– Never understanding why, though...

I'm grimly sticking at the fight,
In a trench, or on barn floors,
From fire-step or empty doorway;
– Never understanding why, though...

When I've asked to be put right
About the point of this butchery,
They've always simply said: '*The Country*...';
– Never understanding why, though...

Better if I just sit tight
And then, when death decides on me,
Slip away and take my leave;
– Still not understanding why, though...

MARC DE LARREGUY DE CIVRIEUX
At the front, February 1916

# 'Everything's so dear...'

*To those who think life is 'dear' and hold the lives*
*of others so cheap*

'Everything's so dear,' civilians bleat;
But I say Life is cheap – never worth less.
For I know a Butcheress
Who's slashed the price of all her meat:
Her Phrygian bonnet splendid red,
Lips fresh and wet with blood she's drunk,
Harlot's eyes in brutish head,
She chucks her stuff out with the junk!

She buys at monstrous markets, then
To the abattoir she dashes
And heavy hammer-blows she smashes
Down on gasping, panting men
That with her massive fists she bashes!

She dismembers, chops and flays
Limbs and trunks from skull to toe,
Then puts the carrion on display,
Labelled 'Prime Quality Hero',
For sale to rat, and worm, and crow!

'Life's expensive,' you maintain?
– Yet all that offal you disdain
That's to be had from the Butcheress!
I say life was never worth less.

Eat! And diligently farm
The Dead, to save the Lives dear bought
Of those who, with unrepentant charm,
Urged them headlong to the slaughter,
To keep their own choice flesh from harm!

Good souls, at love and charity so able,
Save your Consciences with brave litany:
Before you squash in round the table,
Offer up a sumptuous fable,
A prayer to the 'New Trinity',
While observing all the niceties,
In chorus singing 'Benedicite'
At your feasting on Humanity!

Sanctify again that divine resolution,
The sacrifice that saved you from damnation;
And upon yourselves pronounce your absolution,
'In the name of Justice, Right, and Civilisation!'

MARC DE LARREGUY DE CIVRIEUX
On rest, Robert-Espagne, 2 September 1916

# Still Raining...

*To my father, whose 'motherly' letters were always 'fine weather'*

'How like the dead we look, in the glisten
of early, inevitably raining, dawn...
It rained all yesterday, and the day before,
it's been raining, day and night, the whole War!
We look so like the dead, in their misery.'

'The sun was out...' – When? I can't remember...
last year... or the year before, perhaps?
Yesterday? – Rained harder than ever!
Or else I've just forgotten... Can't remember:
　　　　　　　I didn't get a letter.

How lucky you are to have a mother –
the weather's always fine in mothers' letters,
and, in your replies, it's always sunny;
the poor dear things would be so upset
if you didn't always say 'It's sunny.

'No, I've not been cold, and today
there's a swallow twittering away.
I tell you, spring has well and truly come –
Yes, that naughty winter's gone away,
that worried you so much, my dearest Mum!'

– Sweet pleasure, so to lie to those you love,
with the words of every day, the only ones
we truly understand, which never change
and never lose, as they journey on, the love
they bring from the lips that gave them shape.

NOËL GARNIER

# The Stranger

I'm returning from the realm of torment
    Where the king is death.
– I never left it, it's with me always,
    It's waiting at the door.

I don't belong here now. I'm the stranger
    Who doesn't pause and wait;
The guest who checks the time and straightaway
    Turns to set off back.

Ask no questions. You know that any words
    Would resolve into tears;
I keep them locked in my heart with a lurking,
    Ever-restless secret.

Things look as they were, for still I find
    Each thing in its place,
And even now I still can recognise
    Each tree by its shape.

But this strange tuft of grass between bare flagstones
    Is enough to kill the dream,
Recalling everywhere a lasting absence,
    And that we live in endless passing.


    No, Stranger: you must stay awake,
    It is not time yet to come back home.
    Form no attachment to these things,
    Nor stand in contemplation of them,
    Nor allow the memories
    To flood as water in your eyes.

On no account pick that flower,
Nor let that kiss last any longer,
Hold nothing further in your hands.
Do nothing further that might last.
Your heart would all at once empty.
Quick, quick, you have to go.

I'm leaving – though I was never back.
Can this be it, the last farewell?
The world is slippery to my foot.
I sense I never should have looked
So lingeringly into all
       Those faces.

GEORGES CHENNEVIÈRE
1916

## The Wake

That was dead leaves tapping at the window –
keep it shut: perhaps the evening wind
in his wet coat is waiting to blow in.
In he'd come, hands frozen,
and sit down on the stool,
and rain would drip into the stew,
and, from its kennel in the grate,
the fire would fix him with its gaze –
Yes, it's hostile, is the dog of flames,
to these poor wretches off the roads,
with their hands
on their knees, their very soul
in the look in their eyes, shameful,
as though all it showed

were fear – what of, though? –
or remorse, afraid…
It would bark!

And yet this ageing beggar knows
many a story of the roads,
and takes them with him everywhere
in his bag of bad weather, with crusts
of mouldy bread from the gutter…
He knows all about the rain,
the sluggish rivers swollen with hatred
and overflowing…
about the snow, and the frost
on calm, clear nights –
Ah! what if he came in!
He knows about the sky,
and all the sorrows of the earth
trailing in the wind!
What if he came in,
good people at your ease
by that fire that's curled up
lying at your cosy feet…
What if the misery-man came in…

'Go, servants, keep him out!
He smells of death, and soldier…
He says he comforted
our lad as he was dying, and covered him
with dead leaves… No, he's no place here,
this rootless beggar with the evil eye
come to steal our nights.
Lift picks and pitchforks high,
and make it clear
he is to keep away,
this killjoy come to spoil our wake!'

He's gone. Let's eat, for in the pot
the stew is piping hot.
And feed the fire a right good
helping of that light-rich wood!

NOËL GARNIER


# Epistle from a Monkey in the Trenches to a Parrot in Paris

Have you read the paper, little Jacko?
I seem to hear you jabbering away
        – In the comicallest way –
        With all the military rococo
        Of the headlines in the *Écho*:
'Crrr… Crrr… Over by Chrrristmas… The Hun must pay…'
        And planning orgies of brioches
        With flour milled from bones of Boches!
        So there you are, in parrotry
        Mirror to your Matamore
        (E'er the Captain of necrolatry)
        Who, far from eye of Goth and Thor,
        For simpleton lays down the law,
        And signs the column Maurice… Barraggartry!
        Believe you me, I'm proud to know
        So very clever a macaw,
        Who imitates his Master's crow
        And squawks: 'Stand fast!… Esprrrit de corps!'
        – We forest monkeys never show
        Ourselves to men, out in Argonne:
        We have forgotten man, and gone
        More savage than you've ever known!
    'Will out in the flesh what's bred in the bone,'

Any biped hack might echo:
To ape a man is to disgrace your own,
Unless you are a jingoist or Jacko.
So I'll just remain
                    Yours faithfully
                                        *Macaque.*


MARC DE LARREGUY DE CIVRIEUX



## 'The cellar's low...'


The cellar's low; it's like
going into a hotel bar.
The cast-iron pillars support
a mattress of layers of air
and cement.
Acetylene smells like garlic.

Carbousse smells of acetylene.
He knows the Hachette almanac backwards:
ask him anything, he comes up trumps –
the Man with the Axe!
A vile snore-factory,
sighs drowning rolled up in a shipwreck
of blankets.

Brousset grinds his teeth when he's asleep.
It sounds like a wickerwork chair;
when he's awake, he can't do it.
Auguste runs rat hunts
with army revolvers.

I so need to sleep, amongst these gagging
adenoidal battlers; coral
mouths chock-full with dreaming.

My plank and straw. Sleeping bag
buttons at the shoulder.
Float flat on my plank.
Basin.

I'm asleep. I'm not.
Sleep stops on the threshold, I stop
breathing so it'll come in.
A big bird, nervous.

They're all asleep. I'm taming it.
They've all filled up like leaky boats.
And suddenly it's a fleet adrift,
this flotsam of blankets
and knees and elbows.

A foot on my shoulder.
The M.O.'s snuffling, too. Drip, drip,
drop, drip; the basin.
Where are we heading? Shells are falling
on the Hôtel de Ville. They're the bower
we live in.

Rifle fire sharply
slaps on planking.
I would so much like to sleep.
Their poker game's
not helping.

Am I going to have to... Oh, phone.
Hello, hello? Vache crevée farm?
Right, we're on our way. I go up and out.

How long does it take a war
to consume a town? It's a dirty
eater, nutrition by attrition, keeping
one bit back for pudding;
the way a fire will sometimes spare
a net curtain.

I go through the Marines' cemetery. It's an
opium boat, drifting skipperless.
Mast and yards are gone.
Just a tree stump left.
The crew have smoked the cargo; they're all asleep.

The deck's kitted out with what's to be had in Nieuport:
fire dogs, door knobs, candelabras,
wedges for pianos, bricks,
marble mantelpieces,
Madonnas, rings,
glass clock covers.

Tonight, among the ruins, I've heard
the nightingale hard at work.

Who's that braying, coughing, clucking,
croaking, grunting, up in
the chloroformed tree?

It's the nightingale. He's practising
his love song;
and somewhere I can smell – here; there; – no, there!
that scent! it really is!!
it's roses!!!

It's two years since I smelt a rose.
The rose bush, male in bud,
so soon female, packs an explosive scent
that kills the trusting butterflies.

Frilly foreskin roses
indecent in the heat
long ago. Now here I see,
I see a red rose.

I see a cold rose.
How was it allowed in here?

More ferocious than hyena
or raven or vulture –
while they
draw their lustrous black
from the unresting dead
unburied across the plain,
it
hypocritically transmutes
into grace a sombre
greed for the tombs
its pretty mouth
feeds deep from.

JEAN COCTEAU

# Delivering Souls

A cracking place for getting shot,
The Éclusette O.P.
You stepped outside to clear your head
Or puff a pipe; you're dead.

It's simple. Like those dreams
When somebody turns into somebody else
And you don't bat an eyelid.

Death the heavy circus rider
Leaps through you like a hoop.
For stray bullets here
Are birds in a shrubbery
Of iron wire.

This barbed thicket
Is a better soporific than your blue apples,
You chloroform orchards.

The bird swapping cages
Whistles nothing helpful.
For the killer bird
Whines a different path.

Death produces statues –
Blank-eyed, shadow-winged, stone-cold –
With a flick of the wrist.

Like the hare's busy nose,
Life is never still; and, all of a sudden,
Still. Red blood
Runs from the nose down the neck.

If you're sick of fighting,
L'Éclusette's the hide to fight for.
The trick never fails:
Heads is tails.

An old trick, yes,
But done in a flash –
You don't see a thing,
Caught every time.

Enemy, you're such a clever
Conjuror. *Your* revolver, enemy,
Is *your* deliverance, doves.

JEAN COCTEAU


# A Twelvemonth of Grief

So, my country is in peril; my father dead,
    And now my mother.
'Please, no,' I whispered, for the heart is weak – but the mind
    And spirit tough,

And I understood, and no longer wondered
    Why the ones I grieve for
Chose this time for me to watch them lowered
    Into their deep graves.

For, like the blowing pines fiercely holding to these hills,
    More fiercely now
I hold to this soil, the earth I have struck down into
    With both my roots.

EDMOND ROSTAND

# Verdun

Silence shrouds the noblest name on earth:
Verdun, wrapped in endless aftermath.
Here, the men of France came marching, man by man,
One for every second, every day,
To prove the proudest and most stoic love.

Now, the ordeal over, they sleep their last sleep.

Verdun, their immortal widow, trembles and weeps;
Or sobs to heaven above for their return,
Her two high towers like supplicating arms.

Passer-by, think not to extol
The city hosts of angels shielded, sprung
From every inch of France's soil. So much blood
Has run: let no vain human voice ever
Adulterate with feeble, keening pain
The incense misting endlessly from this loam.
Acknowledge, in the slashed and battered plain,
The fathomless and hallowed power of France,
Whose noblest hearts now lie buried in her soil.

The death they died here no word can name,
So consentingly was each man's sacrifice made.

Soaked and sated, earth is made man.
O passer-by, still your voice, stay your hand:
See; feel; pray; revere them for the price they paid.

ANNA DE NOAILLES
November 1916

# A Race for Life

*To Georges Duhamel*

My knees are punching holes in the air,
And my legs are slitting it
Like scissors.
The wind's cold, wet vest
Is clapped to our bellies.

I'm wearing No 15 in an athletics match: the 1200 metres.

I don't like these middle-distance races
That wear down the brain
The way a grindstone wears the knife down.
I'd rather the sudden flare of every muscle,
Crisp,
Brutal, red: the 100 metres.

Each hand clenching a cork
Is what keeps me going;
Chewing on the corner of a handkerchief;
Neck stretched taut –
You could strum it like a mandolin.

I can't keep up with my galloping blood.
My tread's beating time round the track.
I'll pump my whole heart out.
I'll stick at it though, and dutifully
Sweat sinew stress.

The serpent track
Rears its head.
Sink your two fists into the wind,
And let yourself just fall into the wind.

It's intoxicating, on and on,
The steady tread.
The autumn's going to my head.
The cold's a sheath round each thigh.
Chest to chest against the wind,
I'm holding out, on this plain in Picardy,
On this first Thursday in October 1914.

In 1916
I ran another race
And I won,
North of Amiens.

I was holding on to life
The way corpses stubbornly cling to their rifles
With their frozen hands.

I kept falling,
Then up and off again,
My two fists sunk into my stomach.
I was like a punctured barrel.
The wind hissing through my teeth,
My gritted teeth,
My objective
Is a Geneva cross, red on white,
At a crater's edge.
The flagpole's planted in the ground.
The red's washing out in the rain.

The bijou trophy I'm competing for
Is life.
No women to watch us run.
There's one objective:
That flag.
– Two flags suddenly,

Three, four, a thousand flags
From the hands of a swindler who's
Nothing but bones,
And laughing.

I jump the hurdles
Of tangled corpses.
I hear shouting;
The men who can't move,
Stuck, mudbound,
About to die
In their blood-and-mud bath crying out
Spurs me on.
'Don't worry, I'll hold out, I'll make it.'
– And up and off again.

I reached the line.
I'd hardly any blood left in my belly,
But behind the bung of my fists
I'd brought enough back
For surgeons and pretty women
Still to wash their hands in, enough
To live.

MARCEL SAUVAGE

# To Cam

Only for rare, short moments do I ever understand, at last, my dearest
   brother, that you are dead.
For me, you left months ago and I simply think you have been away
   too long,
And I live my life as if I were sure they are holding you there in their
   gloomy forests,
But I believe you will come back on the day when the bugles sound
   our victory.
And I wait for you, and wear no black veils, and when friends' eyes fill
   with pity, I am all stubborn poise.
And they wonder that I can be so brave – but where is the bravery,
   when I still believe you will come back to me,
When I believe that I shall see you walk back in one day through this
   old porch, in the pale blue uniform you wore when you left, that
   last evening?
Together, we had walked out along the path through the peaceful
   fields,
And you, as you often do, had your hand on my shoulder, gentle and
   protective.
And we walked along, as one, in perfect step, as night fell round us.
– And that evening, perhaps, more than ever, was when we felt our
   love's full force.
You left with a smile, and said to us all: 'Back soon!'
– So how should I think you will never come back, when every
   promise you ever made you have kept?
It would be the first time you had ever deceived me…
– And how pointless loving you would be, and how paltry my love,
If it failed to bring you back to me, back from where they say you lie
   amongst the dead!
No one has shown me proof that you are amongst the dead,
And I place no reliance on their flimsy affirmations.
And I sit waiting for you, for there must always be a woman to watch
   the night-light,

Lest the sick man think he is alone and the soul depart the body.

Can you perhaps, if you're still alive, can you perhaps sense the still, small flame

From across the ravaged provinces that lie between us?

Sleep, my silent one; and rest; have no fear for the light, it shan't go out;

I feel I shall wait for you, month in, month out, my whole life long;

When my hair is white, I shall still be hoping to see you walk back in through this porch.

Only for rare, short moments can I ever, sometimes, understand that you are dead.

HENRIETTE CHARASSON
November 1916

# Mobilisation

From men, wild slaves are wrought,
With hobbled limbs and ducking heads;
From women, Vulcan's skivvies, forced
To knead bronze instead of bread.

Wood, rope, leather, glass, coal —
All gone for soldiers. A spate
Of eager coin and gold
Has paid for weapons, man-created

Teeth for man to eat men. The very trees
Are mobilised and piteously deployed,
Wellsprings, hills, the air, the sea —
Today, no man or thing is unemployed.

The players weary — nothing's done by halves,
And he who crosses Nature's like to starve!
We'd best destroy the gardens straight away —
Flowers and lovesome bowers have had their day!

Plough up the lawns, grub out the shrubs and trees,
Forget about providing food for bees.
Sweet lilies, roses, violets demure,
You will all make excellent manure.
Our parks we'll deck with turnip clamps and straw.

Such are the beauties of war.

HENRIETTE SAURET<br>1917

# Ant-Hills

It's here.

The earth is leprosy and iron.
The flooded ruts glisten like rails.
The incessant rain wallows all across the plain.
The wind bites.
Under these flabby swellings
Trenches and ditches
Snake like bowels, burrow, slip away,
Calculated meanders
In the boundless, iron-bristled slime.

On the surface, everywhere,
Corpse.

There, under their monstrous coatings of mud and misery,
Under the gaudy mattresses protecting them
Against freezing cold, streaming water and rampaging air,
There march, eat, sleep,
Joke, excrete,
Men,
Endless ant-hills of men,
Slumped without respite right to the exploding horizon,
Men.

They wait.
They scratch, eaten alive.
They think nothing; they know nothing.
They undergo.

And the ferocious, howling shell
That falls, here, or there,

Throws up a red spout, here, or there –
A batch of corpses.
And, incessantly, they advance, they halt,
They stay, unmoving,
Unknowing, through pale days and acid nights,
Waiting.

The lands are gorged with dead humanity.
The fruit of the earth is corpse.
Its smell spreads out over all the plain.
And each man knows in his heart
That he is future
Corpse.

Yesterday, today... At the appointed hour,
Of the howls, the torrents,
The red and black skies,
The universal heave ripping up and pounding the plain,
The flame, air and earth –
Ordered out, they come out.
They explode, they melt, they live,
They impale flesh and butcher it,
They are possessed with panic bestiality –
Cackles and shouts over rivers of blood,
And it's over.

Behind them, the earth
Is a stinking, gathered meditation of newly dead;
And their wait,
Standing, lying, sprawling,
Resumes.

PIERRE JEAN JOUVE
1917

# The Tank

*[Death speaks]*

My machine, my gift from Mars,
A tower on two jaws,
With human calculation
Alive in its steel skull,
Spitting, from its middle, at the sides and underneath,
Shrapnel, shells, and floods of ravening bullets,
Trampling onward,
Over the ground, over men, the living, the dying, the dead,
Jolting the trenches shut
Like the lips of a wound pinched together,
The armour-plated animal
Crawling on through explosion and battle,
Escaping its very masters –
Inside,
The heroes,
Padded to the eyeballs, thrown against the bulkheads, broken in the
    corners,
Scorched by the engines' torrid heat,
Deafened by the detonations inside the steel,
Living out their last day.

Behold the child of their god-brains,
Behold the light of their arrogant world.

PIERRE JEAN JOUVE
1917

# Somewhere…

Heart pounding, head gone crazy,
I've jumped into a hole, away
Below the cold flow of bullets.
No idea where I am, can't remember.
They said 'Go,' so I went,
As you'd jump into a well.
All round me, the rest,
No idea how many,
All ran shouting and shooting;
Then up in front, suddenly,
A whole impassioned row of good mates,
I don't know, somehow
Started vanishing –
Nine… seven… five… four…
And then two more
I see go down,
And then another
Slumps, dead beat, or dead.
And here's me, on my own,
In the flame and smoke,
Still on my feet, no idea how,
But alive.
It's as though all of my flesh is flopping
Away from the frame of nerve and sinew
That holds me together,
And down I drop into the blackened crater.
Am I scared? No idea –
I'm still past fear,
But I sense it's close,
Just outside my brain,
Ever ready to come back in again.
Flat on my face, I wait for what's to come.

Death? Fear? No idea.
Just what's to come, or could.
Nothing matters here,
My life is dead:
I'm ready for anything or nothing.
The battle's rumbling on,
Like the wind, or a high sea,
With cries, sharper sounds,
Thumps, crackles of iron.
Over my pitiful shell hole,
From left and right
Machine guns sweep
Their fan of drunken bees,
A blade of swarming steel,
Made for scything men
Mathematically.
Now and then the earth erupts.
Memories run through my head,
No idea where from.
My heart is like a sponge, swollen up,
It hurts, I can feel each beat,
Like a clock about to stop.
But does time mean anything
To this pathetic mainspring?
Eternity runs on above my head,
Driven by the hounds of death.
Massive hammer-blows shake the earth,
But in our small sector,
Where suffering's the only winner,
The furnace seems to be dying down.
And, suddenly, there is a silence
More shattering than the din,
A silence all surrounded by the din
Of war to left and right,
A strip of calm beset by whirling hurricanes.

This time, I'm so on my own
I *am* scared, and shivering.
I'm just some poor animal; it feels as if,
Not even stirring, I'm about to leave
And enter all this silence
Waiting to receive me.
My flesh, my soul, are both ice-cold.
Am I even sure I'm still alive?
Perhaps I have already died,
Unawares, thoughts just relics.
I'm incapable of thinking now.
I'm waiting – for what? No idea…
And time trickles on, drop by drop,
Over my defeat, as though distilling
A little eternity.
But now, from the cloud-muffled, low sky,
Here comes pouring rain.
The falling water sounds like bullets,
And every now and then
Furious machine gun squalls skim
Shavings off the flooded plain
In amongst the whirls of rain.
Water's rising in the shell holes.
I'm frozen underneath my cape,
Wetter than I would be naked.
And I'm shivering…
But the rain has given me back
What I'd been abandoned by –
A bit of hope, a bit of energy.
A coward in me has just died,
And I leap into the arms of life.

HENRY-JACQUES
Champagne, May 1917

# Ritornello: The Corporal of France

One night, I shall die a proud Corporal of France,
And beribboned officers, with braid and cane,
Seeing one so young embrace the pain
Of that inscrutable, inflexible ill chance,
Left in speechless envy shall remain.
One night, I shall die a proud Corporal of France.

The gardener, the porter, the slick go-getter,
The infantry recruits, innocents doe-eyed,
The long-since buried, the hard men yet to die,
Shall tearfully unite, each spring, the better
To remember the affectionate despot
Who used to curse them as he poured them out their tots.

May I be survived – faint hoped-for chance –
By Fernand Divoire, André Salmon, Gaston Picard, fine
Flower of all those friends who cherish the arts,
And Urwiller, who gave me fags and wine –
And may these words sing lightly on in your hearts,
If I die, one night, a proud Corporal of France.

GABRIEL-TRISTAN FRANCONI
July-August 1917

# Progress Report

An autumn, and an autumn
yet again;
a summer, and a summer
yet again...
Evil enthroned, guns thundering,
the world nailed fast to an iron gibbet.
The black tree Hate
spreads its sap-dead arms
above the cursed earth
the mad wind roars across.
Humanity has left,
wandering wild,
dragging a dream-dead heart
through vile corpse heaps.
Bitterness and pain,
abortion, death!
The grey of day at times goes coppery,
and the sun grows sick of life
and hides his great gold countenance in night.
Torching monstrous death-throes in the sky
runs War,
gesticulating, screaming, mad,
its shrapnel
shrieking in one endless chant
the curse of flame it casts
on human kind.
Abrupt Golgothas rise and fog the plain,
and at their foot lies dream, crucified,
weeping.
The shades of night spin their skein,
their wheel echoing the ancient dreads.
So tell me:

where lies
the New Humanity?
– For you watched
it soaring through triumphant dawns
towards a dazzling, noble destiny,
glorious,
its young wings stretching heavenwards!
You watched it gliding high above all pain,
godlike,
stars and planets round its head,
– but never saw the thunderbolts, the storms,
the thrashing flails
in skies of suffering.
Too late!
It lived on blood and butchery,
terror after terror, grief upon grief,
manacled the peoples of the earth
and crucified them on gibbets of savagery.
Progress!…
Be silent,
speak no more, my soul.
All
that you can do
is listen
as raging death blasts red through trumpets of flame
and forges hells of murder in the night.

NICOLAS BEAUDUIN

# Undermanned

Ripping saws,
Hissing planes,
Flashing chisels,
Volleys of hammers —

A team three hundred strong,
Ablaze with hectic effort,
One short hour after daybreak
Are knee-deep in shavings.

A thousand crosses for Verdun,
A second thousand for Arras,
Another thousand for Soissons,
And a thousand more for Rheims.

A thousand crosses opening their wings
In fright across the charnel-fields —
A thousand crosses opening their wings
In vain, flight taken prisoner.

Get cracking, carpenters!
– By the time tomorrow's dawn
Has limned the eastern sky,
We'll be needing more, more crosses
For stevedores to stack in ships
Bound for Salonika
And the Bosphorus and Africa.

Faster with the hammers,
Faster with the planes —
We've dropped behind,
Demand's outstripped supply.

Put some beef into it, come on,
We need more crosses –
A good ten thousand to replant
A forest now as bare as heathland;
And two million more to wood
All that disinherited stretch of land
From the Alps to the Channel.

RENÉ ARCOS

## The Dead

The widows' veils
In the wind
All blow the one way.

And the mingling tears
Of the million sorrows riverwards
All flow the one way.

Rank by rank, shoulder to shoulder
The bannerless, unhating dead,
Hair plastered down with clotted blood,
The dead all lie the one way.

In the single clay, where unendingly
The dying and the coming worlds make one,
The dead today are brothers, brow to brow,
Doing penance for the same defeat.

Oh, go clash, divided sons,
And tear Humanity asunder
Into vain tatters of land –
The dead all lie the one way;

For in the earth there remains
But one homeland and one hope,
Just as for the Universe there is
But one battle and one victory.

RENÉ ARCOS

## 'The Gentle Lamb is Risen…'

The gentle Lamb is risen
In lion's guise,
Say the priests of love,

The very Cross a club
That whirls and whirs about our heads.

Somewhere, none knows where,
The Father sleeps his long sleep,
Waking to the Son's cries
Only to dip his idle hands
Into Pontius Pilate's basin.

RENÉ ARCOS

# Of Certain Men

So you'll have saved your skins... Life's glorious!
Not everyone can rot behind some parapet.
'The Republic's calling us,' you chorused,
'We must ensure that she prevail! We'd be no use dead.

'It's right to fight, of course, but rather common –
Our biceps simply aren't the size for holding rifles;
France will need us when the war is won,
And we, far better than in death, shall serve in life.

'The country now needs males, our race needs men,
To impregnate our women in their abandonment.
Our children will be handsome specimens,
Like their sires, us thoroughbred non-combatants.

'While our heroes thaw their broken bodies,
Ruminating on their glory by the fire,
We shall still be youthful, active, bold:
As, for us, they suffered, so we, for them, shall thrive!'

– But we, when we're back (for where there's killing
There will always be a few who do survive),
We shall recuperate our strength and spirit,
And then, perhaps, you'll find us rather too alive.

And should we come across each other, why,
My fine fellows, we'll stop and look you in the eye,
That you might feel, more crimson than hot shame,
Dead soldiers' blood well up and flush your cheeks with flame.

HENRY-JACQUES

# 'And if you delayed...'

*[Addressed to Death]*

And if you delayed, who knows
Whether I myself could not as well
Clear that atrocious barrier
And get myself knocked back flat
Stone dead?

The death of the man who has believed,
The death of the man who scorns,
That is what I would wish
To launch at them like spittle.

PIERRE JEAN JOUVE
1918


# Moments

Come into my arms and cry,
your pain flows all round mine inside me...
'He's fighting...' (Yes, I know, he's fighting.
Better than you, I know he's fighting...
Don't talk about it, don't think about it.)
'He's fighting... The Germans are advancing...
They could be tramping over his smashed head
at this very moment, with us here together.
It's horrible...' Hush... 'I tell you, he's dead.
I can see him lying there... His shadow
makes him bigger. His helmet's full of rain.
– No, it's not, the sun's out... – I'm mad... I am
          mad!... mad!... mad!...'

And then she went to the window
and cupped her face in her hands,
as if to fill them with the misery
from her puffy eyelids.

I went over next to her,
and we looked down into the wet street
at the play of sunlight in the gutters
like a smile through tears.

And the roofs were streaming with light
that fell and crackled on the cobbles
like a storm, and splashed the factory-girls
in their hitched-up skirts...

Walk on, walk on, little girls,
there's sunshine in the street.
If you knew, if you only knew...
Walk on, walk on, little girls...

If you knew, if you only knew
how she suffers... Walk on, walk on,
you'll get time enough yourselves...
All your lives, little girls.

NOËL GARNIER

# Eve of Battle

The clock taps the tip of time into this space
Designed for dream and contemplation, the room
In which, tonight, I wait a wordless wait
As vast armies fight to the conclusion.

To our Vigil, then, solitary haven!
Calm witnesses to each page as I write
Are papers, books, scores, the desk-lamp's light –
But beyond the window panes lies hell.

The violin is here, brushes, canvas,
Books. Is this a woman's brow, intent
Over easel, strings, paper and pen –
Or a soldier looking to his cannon?

In every fold of my simple curtains,
Bombardments, charges, flames and killing rumble.
And, sitting ramrod-straight, I think with fervent
Vigil to save the future of my country.

This poem-hearted sentinel is merely me.
But I feel, I want, I will, I hope, I love;
And perhaps, this night, I shall redeem ignoble
Panics, in defiantly thus facing Fear.

In me is every soldier and civilian
Of our blood, on land, in ships – impassioned,
Battling. It is France I feel in me, her anguish
And her anger, here, thumping in my chest.

I must prevail! Oh, cries of women in the night!
Out there, the men are dying. Oh, the blood, the tears…

Is my tragic clock, the tapping tip of time,
Not telling of our army's victory-cheers?

Paris: silence; love; the nerve to act.
Will the siren start again, and blight
The evening, howling of monsters coming back
To fly at our cathedrals in the night?

No. This night belongs to minds like mine.
We are deep in prayer, in a chapel.
We feel our veins tighten with the blood that binds
Our hearts and France still closer in her peril.

LUCIE DELARUE-MARDRUS
April 1918

# Peticion

Since we are graunted brefe respyte
And all is quieted in the warr,
Captayne, I do thee implore:
Let me languysh here no more,
I faine would see my Love this nyghte.

Naught shall I tell her of our plyght,
If so thou dost enjoyne me: nor
Petards, nor poniards, nor the gore;
Sedulous, I'll trewth ignore –
Her very envy I'll excyte!

Her teres thus dryed, her eies lit bryght
Shall, as I leave, my soule restore.
I'll bidde farewel for evermore,
And, sorrowes soothed, rejoyne the corps
To take up once agayne the Fyghte.

Captayne! Such woes my soule do blyght
As make my herte to beat full sore.
From iron or sobbes, I death abhorre:
Oh graunt me not to dye before
My Love have putte my paine to flyghte!

EDMOND ADAM

# Krieg und Liebe [War and Love]*

Shall I not, today, my sweet, see thee?
I have more love than valour, 'tis remiss.
When I kneel and beg thee for a kiss,
My heart beats never so deliciously!

In my veins my living blood's a-seethe,
Thou art in every wise such bliss.
Shall I not today, my sweet, see thee?
I have more love than valour, 'tis remiss.

This confession, then, receive from me:
For me, this earth holds naught but worthlessness,
My very life but wrack in the abyss,
And senselessness in everything I'll see
Can I not, today, my sweet, see thee!

EDMOND ADAM

# Geschaerfter Stahl [Honed Steel]*

He has a mighty sword he wields with zeal,
And it's made from strongest, purest steel.
Never was a cutting edge so keen –
Just to see it turns a chap quite green.

I'm on my own, but now I sense, I feel
Him, smiling and obliging, closer steal;
He binds my neck in bonds of soft sateen –
If only I were free, I'd flee the scene!

Suddenly, the blade swings down to slice,
And flashes on to me, as cold as ice,
And rips and rasps for what seems half the day.

But I get up at length, and calmly pay,
And bid farewell, and stroll off down the street:
Now and then, a proper shave's a treat.

EDMOND ADAM

* These are two of three poems which, because they were written in German,
were censored en bloc.

# To Myne Censor

*To myne censor, who for no good reason did whole sayle splatte three
doggerels, Germayne onely in the tongue they were writ in*

These humble verses do I dedicayte
To myne censor, who did extirpayte
Sueet nothings that unto my Love I sang –
As well hadde he demanded I shoulde hang –
For 'twas in Germayne I did celebrate.

Scanned they ill, then as their deth-knell rang
In resignacion had I tholed their fate,
And forgiven, not withoute a pang,
    My censor's wrathful cuttes!

In sooth, they spake nor villainie nor hate:
Like flowres, from a gentil soule they sprang,
From love, and from my herte excruciate.
Now, if these present verses he do dang,
Up him shall I them insinuate,
    Where monkies stuffe their nuttes!

EDMOND ADAM

# Gamecocks

I come crawling out of my hole,
my black trench, where the mud
sucks us back.
Neck stretched out I crawl,
not daring raise my head,
temples hot with thudding blood.
I crawl,
and after me my men
come crawling
through the mud,
till they catch in the wire
and it screeches, and skins them
with hatchet fangs,
and clashes on their bayonets.

Rat-tat-tat . . . Zing! Zing!
Lie flat... Rat-tat-tat . . . Zing!
If only we could flatten further.
'They've seen us... They've heard us!'
Bayonet-sharp,
a shudder chills our spines...
My clenched fist clutches my revolver.
And I do just raise my head,
brow and body sweat-soaked.

But they've stopped firing.
We struggle further forward,
crawling... Shh!!
For God's sake make less noise!
Careful with your bayonets.
You over there, come on!
Crack!... Shhwhizzz...
A flare comes climbing to its zenith

and opens out, a blinding flower
over our cringing heads.

Rat-tat-tat!... We can't be seen,
but: Rat-tat-tat-tat-tat!... and: Zing! Zing! Zing!
Boche bastards!
Then blacker night returns,
and we can find a shell-hole
and breathe again.

Ker-rack!... Ker-rack!...
This is horrible!
Zing!... Rat-tat-tat!
For God's sake, Boche bastard,
how long's it going on for,
this machine gun?
Yes, I know: you can see us crawling
towards you.
So, behind your parapet,
you're pumping your mechanical pig.
Wouldn't you just love to smash us...
If you heard us scream, you savage,
wouldn't you just roar: 'Komm, Fritz!
Hör' die Franzosen singen!'
Rat-tat-tat!... Rat-tat-tat!...
But what have we done to you?
We're in the middle of our wire,
*our* wire;
we're going to cut a way right through!
Tomorrow, when we've reached you,
and the raid's on, hell, defend yourself then,
fire then – but not tonight!
just leave us be, we've work to do.

Rat-tat!... Zing!...
All right, you animal,

go on, fire!
That's what you're there for. Fire away!
You're doing your job, like us.
Ker-rack!
We don't give a damn,
fire all you like –
you can't see us, you're firing blind
at the night we're hidden in.
Your pig's spitting in the wind.

I don't really mind, you know.
That's four years now you've been on this job
behind your parapet...
And *we've* been at work for four years, too,
knitting great meshes of entanglement,
then cutting fresh tracks through them, ready
to attack next day and flush you
from your trenches.

Look – your works gates
are next to mine, we're almost mates.
We've been flogging ourselves for rival firms,
each as bad as the other, perhaps –
we can't be sure!
My boss has told me yours
is a villainous, treacherous, murderous,
good-for-nothing swine!
But yours, perhaps,
has said the same of mine.

Anyhow, we're scrapping like dogs,
like gamecocks
with masters relentlessly
and furiously betting one another
and themselves into frenzy;

when it's over, one'll be ruined,
and the other no better off.
And their birds'll have slashed each other
to shreds, feathers and flesh,
and bled to death...

Rat-tat! Rat-tat!
That'll do, old son!
You're stupider than those cocks.
Zing!... Zing!...
You idiot! Don't be stupid!
Rat-tat!... Right, I've had enough!
My master's right,
you're just a brute.
Perhaps you'll kill me.
I've got children and a wife...
Rat-tat! Old son, you're going to pay for this.
I'll skewer you tomorrow, right by your Spandau!
And if you've got a wife,
that's just too bad,
and too bad for your children!
I'm a brute as well,
when I'm pushed too far.

And we'll do as brave gamecocks do, when
they're thrown into the pit at one another,
and unflinchingly, heroically
and ruthlessly fight,
till they drop and die at nightfall of their wounds,
roared on and clapped by an ecstatic crowd,
for the glory, but the ruin too,
alas,
of their unpardonable masters.

EDMOND ADAM
14 May 1918

# Roland Garros

*who escaped the bonds of earth awhile*

The young man already marble
looking out to sea

Columbus a sailor at fourteen

Fréjus ten-minutes' wait        olives
railway-poster blue

He was weaned on maps

A cold water-melon in pink snow

The native so liked the family
he recited compliments on Christmas night

They catch fish in the wavetops
where the big ones sleep

Hunting hummingbirds with limed
bamboo
        Jules Verne

The paradise rainbow tree chirps
we brought whole bunches back

Luggage        Luxury cabin

The Creole women
rolling cigars on their damp thighs

On the first day the sailors bought
cockatoos blue-buttocked monkeys
shaddocks

Dinner-table talk is of the pole

        Ma Paloma

The pirate friend
        Roland's horn
        Tristan's horn

hunting
the Valkyries

The alternating spurting bullets foil
the astral disc of air and wood
Spray      a dervish ghost

      Dear Jean,
*I've killed a* Taube. *What a nightmare. I'll never forget them going
down. They caught fire at 3000 feet. I saw their bodies, bleeding,
horrible. I got a bullet through a longeron in one wing.*

The hero
true hero
inflicts
then pities

How good it will be    up for a flight
               after the storm

Our plan (you remember)

fly low
over deep jungle

A metropolis murmur

The cockatoos intone
charivaris of colour

The musk of swooning boas          wafts up

All Virginia wakens

JEAN COCTEAU


## Medals

War cripples,
With those ribbons and crosses on your chests,
You are heroes, today.

Cripples,
With your ribbons and crosses on your chests,
Tomorrow, for your employers,
You will be less skilled workers,
Paid even less than the rest,
And your children will be hungry.

And if tomorrow, even tomorrow,
We tell you
That you only shed your blood
For your masters to be harsher masters,
You will brandish your stumps at us,
And your crutches of glory and pain,
Cripples, with your ribbons and crosses,
Refusing to accept
That you suffered for nothing.

MARCEL MARTINET

# 'What a man full-grown is...'

What a man full-grown is
I shall say tonight,
In the fire of silence,
In the heart of faith.

He is like the sea,
He has the warm pools
And sightless depths
Where swims a dark idea.

He contains the seasons,
The great waves of winter,
The gulls of springtime,
Summer purity.

Bearing youth, he takes it
From sunlight to sunlight
Down to the depth of death
That is still the sea.

He knows that by some fuddled law
These waters gorge on one another,
But he knows what boundless peace
One drop of water holds.

And the sea is only
Ever a patch of sea,
Bright with Heaven's light
Over slimes in combat.

PIERRE JEAN JOUVE
11 November 1918

# Monday 11 November 1918

The bells are ringing, the bells are ringing,
In these streets, in all these men,
The bells resound, ring out
Over the houses, the factories,
Over fields shuddering in the distance,
Over the mountains and plains,
The bells are ringing, the bells are ringing.

Oh, how pale your face is!
Heart beating as if to burst, is it?
And there's this need to weep,
Like growths of anguish in your throat.

*My* need is to speak, asking
Every man on earth: In God's name
Tell me, is it true it's stopped?
Is it true, they've stopped their murdering?

All you dead, my dead, atrociously dead,
Is it true the whole thing's over,
That I shall never see you again?

Oh, how they ring! How they ring!
How they ring inside the hearts
Of those who know, those who weep!

Oh yes, they've stopped the mutual murder.
But – rejoice? On this ossuary?
How can anyone be happy?

And yet this heart is leaping,
The bells are ringing, the bells are ringing.
O you, my murdered ones, forgive me!

My love is there, in your poor graves,
With you, all with you.

But it's over, but it's over!
Oh, how they ring! How they ring!
O ice-cold dead, please forgive me –
The world, the world is set free!

MARCEL MARTINET


## 'Victory, whose calm gaze...'

Victory, whose calm gaze defends the just,
Who clenched your fist and fought your way through hell –
Despite the shed blood, the betrayal of the trust
And strength of youth into pain and debility,
Despite the scabbing rust of suffering
That clogs and ruts every turn along the way,
I would proclaim your august divinity,
Could I not see, in your other fist,
Like ancient medals in dusty display,
Those human faces rubbed away.

ANNA DE NOAILLES

# Recall-Up

Suppose, all at once,
Blood were to bead
From mahoganies
And walls and hangings
In your drawing-rooms?

Suppose, in the night, all at once
The lamps bled,
Lights like wounds?
Or your rugs swelled and
Exploded, like bellies of dead horses?

Suppose the violins
Took up
The tears of the men,
The last refrain of the men
With exploded skulls across every plain on the globe?

Suppose your diamonds, your bright diamonds,
Now were only eyes
Madness-filled
All round you, in the night,
All at once?

What would you tell of life
To a skeleton, suddenly there,
Stock-still, bone-bare,
Its only mark
A Military Cross?

MARCEL SAUVAGE

# Thou Shalt not Kill

Clocks' hearts
Alone beat
On their own
In the bedrooms.

The lamps have been shot.

In forgotten legends
Gutted houses gape out
Mourning and silence.

The children are dead.
Over corpses rampant grasses
At the wind's whim
Bow and curtsey.

Ten million pounded heads ground
For a grain that will never sprout now,
A grain of wheat that can never sprout now,
One small future-seed, lost…

The lamps have been shot.

MARCEL SAUVAGE

# Result

All down the downward track
Of age runs blood,
Man blood and horse blood.

And the machines' mouths and wheels
Are covered in blood,
All down this downward track

Towards the sea and the setting sun
Of age. A blood of sour mud,
Man blood and horse blood.

MARCEL SAUVAGE

# The Castigation
*To Frédéric Lefèvre*

In the street
The carts
On the cobbles, like clacking rattles,
The taxis racing off,
Red, rear ends smoking.
The tramcars squeal
Under their trolleys.
On the pavements
People walking, walking by, walking on.
Life's strident bellow.
The city: Paris.

Bowling along came a posh
Limousine.

A beast of burden,
A man,
A sweating man
Dragging a handcart,
Got in its way.
A gentleman leaned out
From the posh limousine,
An elderly gentleman of means,
And shouted the following observation
At the poor poverty-stricken devil
Trapped in the swirl of the street:
'You blithering idiot,
Serve you right if you got run over.'

I looked at the man
Who was dragging the handcart.
He said nothing, did nothing.
He had a wooden leg,
He was dragging a heavy handcart,
He was sweating,
He had two medals on his dirty lapel,
The Military Cross,
The Military Medal.
This was yesterday's hero,
A martyr sweating,
Frightened, resigned – yet another
In the swirl of the street,
A beast of burden – yet another
In the swirl of life.
The posh gentleman of means
Should have done him a favour
And run him over,
Poor b——.

MARCEL SAUVAGE

# Consent

'Do you, for all your wordlessness,
At least consent,
Bodiless, unspeaking ghost?

Nothing will I ever do
To give you hurt,
My gentle, loving, sure support.

But I am his, and he is mine,
Until we die;
Give me comfort, unbegrudged.

If your love for me indeed
Was true, make haste:
The One my life is pledged to waits.

I have mourned you one whole year,
And the roses
On your grave have lost their petals.

— Ah! I knew it would be "Yes",
Full-flowering heart,
My hero in Elysium…'

\*

'I come, my love, I come!'

MARCEL SAUVAGE

## 'I think of those...'

I think of those who hugged you, War, like lovers,
And sang your praises like a mistress's;
And those who made you up with paint and powder
    To lure the innocent millions.

I think of those who smiled unwitting smiles
As shuddered, wept and died an entire world;
I think of certain widows in their black veils,
    So very fetching on blonde curls.

CÉCILE PÉRIN

## Homesick for the War

I made mine your mouth and your firm breasts
In a single, sacrilegious kiss;
My torment melted under your caress –
Like sunshine dissipating icy mist.

An emptiness, a horror, fills my head:
Yet again, I have betrayed my dead.

\*

Oh, to bow my head in grief and pain,
Covered in those thousand shrouds again,

Subsisting on no other food
Than blood from all those thousand wounds,

Oh, to bleed, to bleed, as bled
In other times the men I led,

When war, unsated, gluttonous,
Choked my mouth with sand and dust –

Like a corpse down a hole, hopelessly
Chewing the darkness, chewing, endlessly.

MARCEL SAUVAGE

## Young Shades

Limpid Summer evening, swimming
With swallows twisting and swooping,
Tranquil landscape, horizon
Awash with sunshine, blue sky
Lit with yellow plums –
What have you done with all the faces?

The faces of the youthful dead
Dissolved in your fluidity?
The handsome dead, sprung
By the hair-fine triggers of Spring
And the switches and filaments of Summer
Up into the urgent spreading foliage
Of earth's eternity.

Nimble, scintillating sap
That Nature is built from,

What have you done with their dreams,
Lulled in your pulse, lulled in your breathing,
And fulfilled as dew
In the cool, reposing shade?
These dead are the very flesh of day,
They are the fruit, the vine, the wheat,
Their sacred bones, distilled and gathering
Through roots and stalks, now fill and consummate
The spotlessness of space.

But that sweet, terrible love
That all the universe shouts of,
The stir and jubilation of desire,
Arms opening to shuddering gasps,
The ecstasy of tears and fire,
Those high triumphant moments
That no other glory can touch,
When we are Destiny's match
And the spasms inside us
Are beating out a future –
Who shall restore all this to the countless dead?
Who shall restore it to you, poor shades,
In your numberless oneness
Pining in the skies of Summer nights?

ANNA DE NOAILLES

# NOTES ON THE POEMS

**p. 20 Edmond Rostand, 'Burning Beehives'.** Fraimbois is a little village about 30 miles south-east of Nancy. It was occupied by the Germans from 26 August to 11 September 1914, houses ransacked and civilians shot. The village priest complained that his beehives had been set on fire and destroyed, and received the reply from General Danner 'Que voulez-vous? C'est la guerre' ('What do you expect? That's war'). The priest was himself detained for 16 days, on the grounds that shots had been fired at German soldiers in his parish. (My warmest thanks to Thierry Choffat, deputy mayor of Fraimbois, who kindly supplied me with this information.)

The *Fables* of La Fontaine (1621–95) are one of the icons of French culture; the allusion is doubtless to 'Les frelons et les mouches à miel' ('The hornets and the bees'). Plato likens society to a hive in the *Republic*. Vergil's fourth *Georgic* is on bee-keeping. The Belgian playwright Maurice Maeterlinck (1862–1949) wrote a remarkable essay entitled *La Vie des abeilles* (*The Life of Bees*). Pierre de Ronsard (1524–85) is the best-known poet of Renaissance France; rose imagery is central to some of his most famous poems. André Chénier (1762–94) at first supported the Revolution, but later attacked its excesses and was guillotined. In the second of his *Iambes* (*Iambs*), he says that his true voice is honey, not venom, and that when the whole hive of his work is opened, it will be seen that he only turned to satire in defence of peace, the *patrie* and humanity.

Much of the Belgian town of Louvain, including some magnificent medieval buildings and the university library, was burned down by German troops in August 1914, who alleged that it was harbouring snipers.

**p. 28 Jean Cocteau, 'When it's Us "Who Were in the War"'.** Published in the weekly *Le Mot* in January 1915. Vareddes is a village north of the Marne. In September 1914, the German line ran from Puisieux south through Étrépilly and Vareddes. After fierce fighting, the French retook the village on 8 September.

**pp. 31, 32 Edmond Rostand, 'The Cathedral'; Albert-Paul Granier, 'The Cathedral'.** Many poets wrote of the severe damage done to Rheims cathedral by German artillery in 1914. The cathedral has triple symbolic significance: an ancient place of Christian devotion; a magnificent, and in some respects unique, example of French architectural genius; and the place where French kings were crowned.

**p. 34 Guillaume Apollinaire, 'The Bleeding-Heart Dove and the Fountain'.** The 'bleeding-heart dove' has a brilliant red splash on its breast. The people named in the fountain part of the calligram are all artists or writers.

**p. 52 Anna de Noailles, 'To my Son'.** Noailles' son, her only child, was born in 1900. Her husband had been at the front from the outbreak of hostilities.

**p. 53 Edmond Rostand, 'Horizon Blue'.** Unlike the Germans in their field grey, French infantrymen were easy targets in their bright red trousers and royal blue coats. This uniform began to be replaced with the pale *bleu horizon* from mid-1915.

**p. 54 Guillaume Apollinaire, 'Driver Gunner'.** A heavy gun is being hauled by two horses, one of them ridden by the driver. The first calligram represents the trumpet that sounds reveille; the French words are from one of several scabrous songs that soldiers sang to the tune.

**p. 70 Henry-Jacques, 'Possession'.** The 'Labyrinth' was an elaborate German trench system, some of it underground, between Neuville-Saint-Vaast and the Vimy Ridge. In the second Battle of Artois, in May–June 1915, the French eventually took it, though at great cost.

**p. 71 Guillaume Apollinaire, 'Earth Ocean'.** The shell-churned battlefield was often compared to a motionless sea. The waves are 'chalky' because the bedrock in Champagne, where Apollinaire was fighting, is chalk.

**p. 72 Guillaume Apollinaire, 'What's Where'.** The 'sausages' are sausage-shaped observation balloons.

**p. 81 Albert-Paul Granier, 'The Attack'.** This poem describes the first four days of what turned out to be the battle of Verdun. Both the Bois des Fosses and the Bois d'Hardaumont, north and north-east of Verdun respectively, had fallen to the Germans by 26 February. At the time of writing, of course, Granier had no idea that the battle would last until December.

**p. 83 François Porché, 'The Poem of the Trench'.** Dedicated to Maurice Barrès, this poem is 671 lines long, and divided into three parts: 'La veille' ('The day before'), 'Le jour' ('The day') and 'Le lendemain' ('The day after'). It describes the build-up before an attack by French infantry, the attack itself, and the aftermath. An extract from the second part, and the whole of the third, are given here.

**p. 110 Marcel Martinet, 'The Ladies Speak'.** Henri Barbusse was the socialist author of one of the most famous novels of the war, *Le Feu (Fire)*, a shocking account of life at the front, which shared the prix Goncourt in 1916. Andreas Latzko's anti-war novel, *Menschen im Krieg (People in the War)*, was published in Switzerland in 1917. Extracts were printed in a number of French anti-war periodicals.

**p. 116 Henriette Sauret, 'The Ladies' Peace'.** Margaret of Austria (1480–1530), aunt of Charles V, the Holy Roman Emperor, was regent of the Netherlands. Louise of Savoy (1476–1531), the mother of Francis I of France, ruled when he was absent. The two women negotiated the Peace of Cambrai in 1529, which brought a temporary pause in the wars between France and the Habsburg Holy Roman Empire.

**p. 118 Marc de Larreguy de Civrieux, '"Everything's so dear…"'.** 'Phrygian bonnet' is an allusion to the red 'bonnet phrygien', modelled on headgear worn by the ancient Phrygians, that was worn as a symbol of Liberty by militants in the French Revolution. It was adopted as the symbol of the Republic. 'Marianne', the personification of the Republic, is always shown wearing a Phrygian bonnet.

**p. 124 Marc de Larreguy de Civrieux, 'Epistle from a Monkey in the Trenches to a Parrot in Paris'.** Larreguy was particularly hostile to the armchair generals of Paris, journalists and poets alike; the 'Maurice Barraggartry' in this poem is Maurice Barrès.

**p. 125 Jean Cocteau, 'The cellar's low…'.** In *Discours du grand sommeil*. The Hachette almanac was a periodical compendium of information, a bit like *Pears' Cyclopaedia*.

**p. 129 Jean Cocteau, 'Delivering Souls'.** In *Discours du grand sommeil*. In a letter to his mother, Cocteau refers to a French listening-post in the Éclusette sector as being three metres from a German one.

**p. 144 Gabriel-Tristan Franconi, 'Ritornello: the Corporal of France'.** Fernand Divoire, André Salmon and Gaston Picard were prominent figures on the literary and artistic scene in Paris before the war; Divoire wrote the preface to Franconi's collected poems, published in 1921.

**p. 155 Edmond Adam**, 'Peticion'. One of the mock-archaic poems; published July–August 1918.

**pp. 156–157 Edmond Adam, 'Krieg und Liebe' and 'Geschaerfter Stahl'.** Censored en bloc in June 1918. Published December 1918, in the anti-war periodical *Soi-même*.

**p. 158 Edmond Adam, 'To Myne Censor'.** Published in *Les Humbles*, July 1918, this was Adam's response to the censor, who had cut the three poems in German from the June issue. The censor's own response was to cut the last three lines of this poem!

**p. 159 Edmond Adam, 'Gamecocks'.** Two substantial sections were cut by the censor: from 'Look – your works gates' to 'and bled to death...', and the last twenty lines.

    'Komm, Fritz! Hör' die Franzosen singen!': Come and hear the Frenchmen singing, Fritz!

**p. 163 Jean Cocteau, 'Roland Garros'.** In *Le Cap de Bonne Espérance*. Garros was a national hero, an aviation pioneer. He took Cocteau up for flights in 1914. He made the first flight across the Mediterranean, taking off from Fréjus, in September 1913. In 1914–15, he collaborated with Morane and Saulnier in developing a deflector which permitted a machine-gun to fire through the airscrew arc of an aeroplane without damaging the propeller ('the astral disc of air and wood'). Shot down in 1915, he escaped from prisoner-of-war camp in 1917. He was killed in October 1918, after the poem was written, but before it was published. Garros was from Réunion. His exotic origins are reflected in much of the imagery of the poem.

    P. Vidal de la Blache was the author of the standard geography textbooks used in schools.

    'Ma Paloma' could be an allusion to any of a number of popular songs, redolent of romantic Latin American exoticism; one, 'La Paloma', begins with the protagonist sailing from Havana. The Spanish word 'paloma' means 'dove'; the *Taube* ('dove') was a type of German aircraft.

# NOTES ON THE POETS

**EDMOND ADAM (1889–1918).** Adam volunteered for active service in 1914. He was killed in August 1918. He was an adventurous writer, skilled in various manners. His first published poems (1918) were mock translations from pre-Islamic Arabic. These appeared in the May issue of *Les Humbles*, a literary magazine hostile to the war. The June issue was to have contained four poems by him. Three were in German, and for that very fact suppressed by the censor. The fourth, heavily censored, was 'Coqs de combat' ('Gamecocks'). At the same time, Adam published satirical anti-war texts in mock-archaic French. Although hostile to the war, Adam was no shirker: he was twice mentioned in dispatches and made a Chevalier de la Légion d'Honneur.

**GUILLAUME APOLLINAIRE (1880–1918).** Born Wilhelm de Kostrowicki, he was the illegitimate son of a Pole and (probably) an Italian. Apollinaire moved to France in his teens, but did not become a French citizen until war had broken out. The uncertainties of his civil status may partly account for the turbulence of his work, both pre-war and wartime, by turns comic, maudlin, fragmentary, recondite, down-to-earth, traditional and revolutionary. Most of his war poetry was published in 1918, in *Calligrammes (Calligrams)*. It exhibits the same openness to the most diverse impressions, the same fluidity and play of simultaneities and, sometimes, the same classical qualities, as his other work. *Calligrammes* also sees the introduction of picture poems, in which the plastic layout of the text has a variety of relationships with the linguistic sense, sometimes reinforcing it, sometimes extending or even contradicting it. Apollinaire was in the artillery at first. 'Driver Gunner', 'The Bleeding Heart Dove...', 'The Horseman's Farewell' and 'Festival' were written during this period. In November 1915 he obtained a transfer to the infantry: 'Earth Ocean' and, perhaps, 'What's Where' reflect the experience of the trenches. Apollinaire received a serious head wound in 1916. He could not return to the front, but the last two years of his life were very creative and influential, in many domains. He died in the influenza epidemic of late 1918, weakened by his wound and the lasting effects of poison gas.

**RENÉ ARCOS (1891–1959).** Like Jules Romains, Arcos was one of the pre-war Groupe de l'Abbaye (1906–1908), a community of writers and artists with unanimist sympathies, but hostile to the alienation forced on the individual by modern society (see notes to Romains). He was invalided out of the army early in the war, and became increasingly *persona non grata* with the authorities because of his anti-war journalism. The poems translated here were not published until 1919, in *Le Sang des autres (The Blood of Others)*.

**NICOLAS BEAUDUIN (1881–1960).** Before the war, influenced by Whitman, Verhaeren and Marinetti, Beauduin wrote poetry expressing a fervent desire to lose the self in a kind of universal super-being. At the outbreak of war, he abandoned these experiments for an incantatory style in traditional verse, the cosmic self-transcendence replaced by an equally passionate surrender of himself to France. A serving soldier, Beauduin was one of those who saw France as chosen by God to save culture and civilisation. The first two poems translated here are from *L'Offrande héroïque* (*The Heroic Offering*), published in 1915 and dedicated to the fallen – and also, be it noted, to Maurice Barrès. A different note is sounded in 'Progress Report', written in November 1917 but not published until 1919.

**HENRIETTE CHARASSON (1884–1972).** Throughout her career, Charasson's poetry was for the most part a limpid, confident celebration of domesticity, motherhood and childhood, a celebration informed by an apparently simple Christian faith. She is not a complacent writer, however, as is clearly seen in *Attente* (*Waiting*), a book of war poems written between 1914 and 1917, in which she expresses a gamut of emotions from hope to fear to uncertainty and even, sometimes, religious doubt and revolt. The book is dedicated to her brother Camille, who was posted missing in September 1915, and never returned.

**JEAN-PIERRE CALLOC'H (1888–1917).** A militant Catholic and Breton nationalist, Calloc'h volunteered for the front as soon as the war started, seeing it as a defence of civilisation and Christianity – only Ireland and Brittany, he writes in a pre-war poem, still help Christ carry the Cross. He was fearsome in attack, armed with a sailor's boarding axe. He was killed by a shell in April 1917. His earliest writings were in French, but from about 1905 he wrote in Breton, often translating his poems into French. His own selection of what he thought his best texts was published in 1926. 'Veni, Sancte Spiritus' is translated from his French. Where this differs from the Breton, I have tried to follow the Breton; I would not have been able to do this without the help of Dr H. Ll. Humphreys, whom I cordially thank.

**GEORGES CHENNEVIÈRE (1884–1927).** Chennevière (the pen name of Léon Debille) was a close friend of Jules Romains, and collaborated with him in developing the notion of unanimism and in writing a treatise on versification (see note on Romains, below). Chennevière's pre-war poetry often expresses the joyous rediscovery of self in communion with others, although there is sometimes a friction between the uniqueness of self and the reality of the 'unanime' which contradicts it. This tension is especially clear in some of the war poems, which reflect Chennevière's experience in the infantry; they were published, together with his pre-war poems, in 1920.

**PAUL CLAUDEL (1868–1955).** A professional diplomat, Claudel was also a dramatist who revolutionised poetic theatre in France, and an eloquent and innovative poet. He is one of the major Christian writers of twentieth-century France. Seeing that written prose, like orthodox verse, is an artificial distortion of natural speech rhythms, he developed free verse into what he called 'versets', each line resembling something like a biblical verse; nor was he afraid to introduce colloquial syntax, preferring expressive vigour to bookish contrivance. As a diplomat, Claudel spent most of the war abroad. His war poetry is both typical and atypical. It is typical of the patriotic Christian; atypical in that such poetry was usually written in mediocre, old-fashioned verse. Claudel's Great War poems were collected as *Poèmes de Guerre* in 1922. 'For as Long and as Often as You Wish, Sir!' was written and published in 1915; 'The Precious Blood' was written in 1915 and published in 1916.

**JEAN COCTEAU (1889–1963).** Cocteau is best known for his plays, films and novels, but he always called himself a poet, and he published several volumes of poetry. To some he is a mythomaniac poseur, to others an inventive leader of the avant-garde; some of the poems given here might lend themselves to either view. Unfit for active service, Cocteau worked with a volunteer medical unit in 1914. Then he joined a Red Cross unit and was posted to Coxyde, near Nieuport (Belgium), in December 1915. Apart from spells in Paris and Boulogne, he stayed there until posted to the Somme in June 1916. He subsequently had a desk job at Military Headquarters in Paris, and was on sick leave from July 1917 until the end of the war. *Le Cap de Bonne-Espérance* (*The Cape of Good Hope*), published in 1919, was written in part while Cocteau was at the front, and finished in 1917. *Discours du grand sommeil* (*Spoken From the Great Sleep*), written in 1916–1918, published in 1924, is entirely inspired by Cocteau's experiences at the front, which he often described as dreamlike.

**LUCIE DELARUE-MARDRUS (1880–1945).** As well as a poet and novelist, Lucie Delarue-Mardrus was a painter and a violinist. Her pre-war poetry is characterised by an exultant physical and spiritual communion with the seasons and the natural world in general, and with her native Normandy in particular. For the first few months of the war she worked as a Red Cross nurse, but found the work too tiring on top of her journalism. All Delarue-Mardrus' war poems are included in *Souffles de tempête* (*Gale Blasts*), 1918. To judge from her memoirs, 'All Souls' Day' was probably written in November 1915. 'Eve of Battle' is the first of a set of eight poems dated April 1918, which together constitute 'The Big Offensive'.

**GABRIEL-TRISTAN FRANCONI (1887–1918).** Called up into the artillery in 1914, Franconi chafed at being too far from the action. He got himself transferred to the infantry. Wounded in 1916, when he came out of hospital he applied, without success, to serve in aircraft or tanks. He was mentioned many times in dispatches and decorated four times. He was killed in July 1918. His best-known work is the novel *Un Tel de l'armée française* (*A.N. Other of the French Army*); Un Tel is Franconi's mouthpiece, passing energetic judgement on everyone and everything, military and civilian alike. Franconi's poems were published in 1921.

**NOËL GARNIER (1894–1931).** Several times wounded in battle and decorated, Garnier expresses his sometimes visionary opposition to the nightmarish war in a mixture of love for his dead mother, whose Christian faith has been rendered obsolete by the war, of affection and pity for his comrades (theirs is the true crucifixion), and of angry attacks on *bourrage de crâne*. Most of these poems were published in 1920, in *Le don de ma Mère* (*My Mother's Gift*); 'Still Raining', 'The Wake' and 'Moments' are from this collection. The other poems translated here are from a section entitled 'Forgetting the Dead' in *Le Mort mis en croix* (*The Dead Man Crucified*), published in 1926.

**ALBERT-PAUL GRANIER (1888–1917).** A solicitor in Brittany, Granier was called up in the artillery when war broke out. He was killed in action as an artillery observer in aircraft. *Les Coqs et les Vautours* (*Cockerels and Vultures*) is his only published poetry. First published in 1917, it was long forgotten in France before being rediscovered and republished in 2008. These are not the poems of a jingoist or militarist, but of a lover of ideas and the arts who is now constrained to hate. Granier nonetheless often makes clear his commitment to the defence of his country.

**HENRY-JACQUES (1886–1973).** Henry-Jacques is the pen name of Henri Edmond Jacques, sailor, journalist and writer. An army reservist, he was called up at the outbreak of war and was twice seriously wounded, in 1915 and 1916. After serious illness in 1917, he was invalided out of the army. He was decorated with the Croix de Guerre and made an Officier de la Légion d'Honneur. His war poems were published in 1918, in *Nous... de la Guerre* (*Us in the War*), and 1921, in *La Symphonie héroïque* (*The Heroic [Eroica] Symphony*). All the poems here are from *Nous... de la Guerre*.

**PIERRE JEAN JOUVE (1887–1976).** In exile during the Second World War, Jouve combined spirituality and humanist patriotism in powerful Resistance poems. During the Great War, however, he was fiercely pacifist, most of his work being published in Switzerland because of its anti-war message. At first, medically unfit for service, he had volunteered as a hospital nurse; falling dangerously ill, he went to Switzerland for treatment in late 1915. While there, he wrote and lectured as a militant pacifist. Like many of the anti-war poets, Jouve speaks as a lone and rejected prophet. *Vous êtes des hommes* (*You are Men*) was the only volume of Jouve's war poetry to be published in France, in 1915. 'For my Immeasurable Love' is from this collection. 'Ant-Hills' and 'The Tank' are from *Danse des morts* (*Dance of the Dead*), published in Geneva in 1917; throughout, gleeful commentaries are spoken by Death. The remaining poems are from *Heures. Livre de la Nuit* (*Hours. The Book of Night*), published in Geneva in 1919 and informed by a temptation to reject the bellicose 'ant-hill' of humanity and to live in communion with God.

**MARC DE LARREGUY DE CIVRIEUX (1895–1916).** Larreguy was born into an old conservative family, and was for a while in the right-wing *Action française* movement. From the time he went to the front in July 1915 to his death at Verdun in November 1916, however, his opposition to the war grew continuously. Larreguy's poems were published in 1920, as *La Muse de Sang* (*The Muse of Blood*).

**MARC LECLERC (1874–1946).** A journalist, poet and artist, Leclerc was an enthusiastic promoter of the dialect and culture of Anjou. He wrote and anthologised poetry and stories in Angevin dialect, sometimes in collaboration with Angevin painters. He also put together a collection of old maps of Anjou, though this was not published until after his death. *La Passion de notre Frère le Poilu* (*The Passion of our Brother the Poilu*), published in 1916 and reprinted many times, is written in the language of an uneducated, small-time Angevin farmer. I have translated it into a vaguely Midlands-of-England passe-partout idiom, in the hope that readers will feel free to substitute whatever regional features they are most familiar with.

**ANDRÉ MARTEL (1893–1976).** A teacher, Martel was mobilised in 1914 and posted to the Argonne. Wounded and buried alive by a German mine in 1915, he was invalided out of the army after 17 months in psychiatric hospitals. *Poèmes d'un poilu 1914–1915* (*A Poilu's Poems*), published in 1916, exhibits a wide range of tones, exemplified by the poems in this selection. All the poems given here are from *Poèmes d'un poilu 1914–1915*.

**MARCEL MARTINET (1887–1944).** An internationalist and socialist, Martinet was a local government officer in Paris. As the war went on, Martinet, who was exempt from military service, entered into contact with leading opponents of the war at home and abroad. He expressed his anti-war views in a series of passionate poems, *Les Temps maudits* (*Cursed Times*), from which all the poems given here are taken. This was banned by the French censorship, so it was published in Switzerland, in 1917. An expanded edition was finally published in Paris in 1920.

**ANNA DE NOAILLES (1876–1933).** Anna, comtesse de Noailles, was a popular figure both socially and artistically. Her pre-war poetry expresses a monistic celebration of life and living. Some of her war poetry gives voice, grandiloquently but never hysterically, to the patriotic clichés of the time. But much of it is more subtle than that, expressing tensions between patriotism and scepticism, between triumphalism and discretion (or even despair), between a need to put the war into words and a realisation that words are not up to it. All the poems translated here are from *Les Forces éternelles* (*The Eternal Forces*), 1920.

**CÉCILE PÉRIN (1877–1959).** Périn's poetry typically expresses gently sensuous acceptance of the pleasures of the natural world and domestic life. In *Les Captives* (*Captive Women*) of 1919, however, while it is unmistakably Périn's voice that is heard, a note of anguish and sometimes of incipient protest is struck. The volume exemplifies specifically female reactions to the war which are to be found in many other women poets.

**FRANÇOIS PORCHÉ (1877–1944).** Despite his age and a heart condition, Porché was called up at the outbreak of war and served in the infantry until December, when he was invalided out of the army. He had published poetry before the war, and then in 1916 poems on the Battle of the Marne; but it was *Le Poème de la tranchée* (*The Poem of the Trench*) that in that same year made him one of the best-known soldier-poets of the war.

**JULES ROMAINS (1885–1972).** Primarily known as a novelist and comic playwright, Romains (born Louis Farigoule) was first known as a poet and as the founder of unanimism. This movement, with which Arcos, Chennevière and Jouve were also associated, postulated that groups of people, however defined, had a collective soul or spirit which conditioned individual members' behaviour. Unanimism marked much of Romains' subsequent work, above all *Les Hommes de bonne volonté* (*Men of Goodwill*), a 27-volume novel (1932–1946) of which two volumes, *Prélude à Verdun* and *Verdun*, are striking representations of the war (although Romains had no experience of combat). Romains' war poems were collected in *Chants des dix années* (*Songs of the Ten Years*), published in 1928.

**EDMOND ROSTAND (1868–1918).** Rostand is best-known for his verse theatre, above all *Cyrano de Bergerac*. His war poetry is gathered in *Le Vol de la Marseillaise* (*The Flight of the Marseillaise*). When war broke out, he conceived this work as a single vast poem, opening with the *Marseillaise* taking wing in Strasbourg (where it was composed in 1792) and returning there after liberating the peoples. He was unable to finish it before his death. Thematically, it is typical of the great majority of patriotic poetry of the war: synonymous with Grace, both aesthetic and theological, France has been chosen by God to save civilisation. Thematically and stylistically, the poems translated here are good examples of Rostand's most typical modes in *Le Vol de la Marseillaise*.

**HENRIETTE SAURET (1890–1976).** Sauret's pre-war poetry expresses delight in living and in creativity. In *Les Forces détournées* (*Forces Misused*) of 1918, however, the abused 'forces' are both the physical forces of the natural world and the human ability to use them in science, technology, philosophy and art; all the poems given here are from this collection. *L'Amour à la Géhenne* (*Love in Gehenna*) of 1919 is more of an exploration of the private 'torture' of lovers separated by the war. Her writing is uneven in tone and quality, but she still makes her points clearly enough for six of the poems in *Les Forces détournées* to have been severely cut by the censor.

**MARCEL SAUVAGE (1895–1988).** A soldier-poet hostile to militarism, Sauvage was seriously wounded on the Somme. The poems translated here were written between 1916 and 1920, and republished in *À Soi-même accordé*, © Éditions Denoël, 1938.

**HENRI-CHARLES THUILLIER (1867–1928).** Thuillier was the village priest of La Neuve-Lyre, in Normandy. Among other initiatives, he set up an annual poetry competition which put the village on the map nationally. Most of his own war poetry was published in *Lauriers de Lyre* (*Laurels of Lyre*) in 1923, and in a set of playlets for performance by children, published in 1917, *Roses France* (*A France of Roses*), both republished in 2014 by Nigel Wilkins. These books bore the legend 'Dieu et France' ('God and France') on their cover, reflecting Thuillier's wish to move beyond the friction between secular and ecclesiastical authorities consequent on the separation of Church and State in 1905.

# THE TRANSLATOR

Ian Higgins has published widely on French poetry of the two World Wars and on translation. With his co-author, the late Sándor Hervey, he originated the ground-breaking *Thinking Translation* series of undergraduate/postgraduate textbooks (Routledge). Among his translations are: André Verdet, *Chagall's World* (The Dial Press); Pierre Seghers, *Piranesi* (Forest Books); *Jacques Rozenberg, a Tribute: Painting and Thought* (Andrée Caillet-Rozenberg); *Florilegium*, texts by Francis Ponge with engravings by Jane Kennelly (Epsilon); prose and verse by nine writers in *The Lost Voices of World War I*, ed. Tim Cross (Bloomsbury); poems by French writers in *We Are the Dead – Poems and Paintings of the Great War, 1914–1918*, ed. David Roberts (Red Horse); and, most recently, Albert-Paul Granier's incomparable Great War poems, *Cockerels and Vultures* (Saxon Books).

# Minds at War
## Poetry and Experience of the First World War
### Edited by David Roberts

**This groundbreaking and long established anthology** of First World War poems will appeal to people who wish to get to know both key poets and poems that everyone should encounter but also read more widely and gain a deeper understanding of both the poetry and the mindsets of people caught up in the First World War.

It includes the great classic poems of the war, poems by many women poets, and unfamiliar poems that are important because they enjoyed huge popularity at the time they were written. The poems are set in their historical context, with many revealing insights from diaries, personal letters and accounts, pronouncements by the media, politicians and others.

**This volume includes** 250 poems by 80 poets, contemporary photographs and cartoons, maps, biographies, glossary and bibliography. *Minds at War* is an illuminating, fascinating, and moving anthology, one of the largest of First World War poetry. It is widely used in academic institutions in Britain and America.

"My students are devouring it faster than I can assign readings. This is a great collection." – Thomas H Crofts, Assistant Professor of English, East Tenessee State University.

"Minds at War is no mere anthology but a comprehensive overview of the poetry and experience of the First World War. It includes the poets and poems one would expect to find plus a number of lesser practitioners and some outright surprises. David Roberts sets the poems and the poets' lives within a contextual commentary which keeps the story of the war moving forward and provides as many useful historic insights as poetic." - Peter Carter, *The John Masefield Society Newsletter*.

410 pages    9"x 6"    Paperback    Illustrated    Ninth printing
ISBN 978-0-9528969-0-6      £15-99 (UK)
## Saxon Books
warpoetry.co.uk

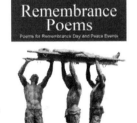

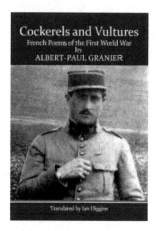

# Cockerels and Vultures

## Les Coqs et les Vautours

### ALBERT-PAUL GRANIER

**For almost 90 years** this outstanding French poet of the First World War was unknown in his own country. The chance finding of a slim and musty little volume of his poetry at a jumble sale in France in 2008 was a revelation to the finder. Granier was soon republished in France and astonished French readers.

Though he is stylistically very different, some compare Granier with Guillaume Apollinaire, and Granier stands comparison with the best of British war poets.

Now English-speaking readers can encounter this remarkable talent through Ian Higgins' fine translation.

***Cockerels and Vultures*** is a book for everyone interested in the poetry of the First World War.

**Albert-Paul Granier** was born in 1888 in Le Croisic, on the Atlantic coast of Brittany. He was a talented sportsman, musician and poet. He qualified as a solicitor, but, from 1911 to 1913, he was required by compulsory national service to serve in the army, where he trained as an artillery officer. He was recalled to the army in August 1914 and served on the Western Front. He became an airborne artillery observer and was shot down and killed over the battlefields of Verdun on 17 August 1917. His volume of war poetry, *Les Coqs et les Vautours,* had just been published in Paris.

**The Translator**
Since the dramatic rediscovery of Albert-Paul Granier, the translator, Ian Higgins, has been in close contact with the poet's surviving relatives, and is uniquely placed to introduce this remarkable writer to English-speaking readers.

90 Pages    7.5"x 5"    Paperback
ISBN 978-0-9528969-7-5    **£9-95 (UK)**
## Saxon Books

www.warpoetry.co.uk